SUNDAY ADELAJA

INSULTED
BY
UNGODLINESS

Sunday Adelaja
Insulted By Ungodliness:
Raising a generation
of the provoked in every nation

©2016 Sunday Adelaja
ISBN 978-1-908040-40-4

Copyright © Golden Pen Limited
Milton Keynes, United Kingdom. All rights reserved
www.goldenpenpublishing.com

Cover design by Alexander Bondaruk
Interior design by Olena Kotelnykova

© Sunday Adelaja, 2016,
Insulted By Ungodliness: Raising a generation
of the provoked in every nation — Milton Keynes, UK:
Golden Pen Limited, 2016
All rights reserved.

CONTENTS

PREFACE

In our world today, godliness is steadily becoming an uncommon thing and people are gradually becoming uncomfortable with godliness. What do you see then? Ungodliness is fast becoming the norms in many societies and this is a common phenomenon in different nations of the world. Therefore, there is a need for a new set of people to arise, those who will see ungodliness as a direct insult and assault on them. They are going to be uncomfortable with ungodliness and insulted by the same.

Many individuals have made so much effort to bring change to their society while many others are not concerned. In most societies today, people are refusing to be challenged by the ungodliness that is rampant. In other words, they refuse to be provoked into things that build the nation and develop society.

The fact is that, in every silence, the neglect and unconcerned attitude towards ungodliness will eventually entrench the practice and the institution of ungodliness in the society. This is part of what every individual with purpose will have to reason out, if there is going to be a change through those who want to make a difference.

People who are insulted by ungodliness are those who eventually change their nation. These are the people who make a difference in their world. Somehow, God has a way of using insults to build something constructive. God has a way of having His way with our anger.

Malala Yousafzai would not sit down and watch how the Pakistani radical Muslims deprived girls the right to formal education. For years, the Taliban destroyed schools where girls studied on a daily basis.

Despite her tender age, Malala would not compromise with her conscience. She started her campaign against the Taliban group at the age of 11. She was frustrated and converted it into action. She started a movement whereby she began to speak for the rights of girls to go to school.

When the Taliban announced that from the 15 January 2009, no girl would be allowed to go to school in her Swat Valley part of Pakistan, she got so irritated and angry that she defied the ban and boldly declared "they cannot stop me...our challenge to the world around us is: save our school, save our Pakistan, save our Swat."

The force of Malala's passion was just too much for the might of the Taliban. Her defiance, her doggedness and her persistence made them to organize an attempt on her life in the year 2012. Luckily for her she survived. Today, the example of Malala has become a wonderful story of inspiration to people worldwide of how we should never be indifferent to the wrongs in our society.

It is time to live in the society with a mindset of, one for all, and all for one, young or old, male or female. This is the pattern and the way the good fight and the civilised fight against ungodliness will be fought. Then, in this way, the weak and the mighty would no longer be pummel by the ungodliness in the society. This is the way out for all, since we have all been insulted by ungodliness one way or the other. What is only left for you to do is simple; speak out, stand up and turn your anger into a positive means in order to bring one thing to the society, which is change, change and change for good.

CHAPTER ONE

INSULTED BY INJUSTICE

INSULTED
BY INJUSTICE

What right do you think 'Boko Haram' in Nigeria have to put an embargo on Western education, both for male and female? This terrorist group have continuously displayed effrontery by killing human beings in their countless thousands in northern Nigeria, in the name of their own ideology, which opposes every other civilized ideology. It is therefore normal for the whole of your being to revolt at such barbaric ideology. In other words, what makes you feel like vomiting or what makes a godly anger to rise within you is what these individuals are demonstrating with impunity. You have simply been insulted; your godly belief and your godly philosophy of life have just been dragged in the mud.

What would you do when you have been insulted by ungodliness and injustice right in your face?

This next story should give you an idea and be a pattern for you and to help you in such situations. It is the story of a man called Moses; a man who was preserved by God, the same God who also brought him from being a fugitive and a wanderer in the desert to be a deliverer for His people, the Israelites. In this chapter, we will look at the root and patterns of what it looks like to be insulted by ungodliness.

Moses spent almost forty years of his life serving the people of God. He carried them in his heart and tenderly cared for them with all meekness, to the extent that it was written in his 'testimonial' that he was the meekest man on the surface of the earth.

However, on one fateful day, this meekest man had his godliness insulted. How? The people he had tenderly cared for; interceded for; shepherded for most part of his adult life have gone after an idol - the worship of a golden calf. Moses first heard of their revelling when he was on the mountain in the presence of the LORD.

Moses, with the commandments written on the tablets of stone, saw the people worshipping the golden calf. When he saw this immoral activity, his holy anger was aroused. Immediately, he broke the tablets of stone on the ground.

Moses was so insulted by ungodliness that he commanded to have the golden calf be grinded to powder form and made the children of Israel drink the water. He also commanded the sons of Levi to join him in the fight against this ungodliness and injustice done against the commandments of the LORD. It was recorded that about three thousand men were slain that day by the sons of Levi in obedience to Moses. Moses simply stood on the side of the Lord to fight for His commandments and principles.

> *"And it came to pass, as soon as he came nigh unto the camp, that he saw the calf, and the dancing: and Moses' anger waxed hot, and he cast the tables out of his hands, and brake them beneath the mount. And he took the calf which they had made, and burnt it in the fire, and ground it to powder, and strawed it upon the water, and made the children of Israel drink of it.*
>
> *And Moses said unto Aaron, What did this people*

unto thee, that thou hast brought so great a sin upon them? And Aaron said, Let not the anger of my lord wax hot: thou knowest the people, that they are set on mischief. For they said unto me, Make us gods, which shall go before us: for as for this Moses, the man that brought us up out of the land of Egypt, we wot not what is become of him. And I said unto them, Whosoever hath any gold, let them break it off. So they gave it me: then I cast it into the fire, and there came out this calf. And when Moses saw that the people were na-ked; (for Aaron had made them naked unto their shame among their enemies:)

Then Moses stood in the gate of the camp, and said, Who is on the LORD's side? let him come unto me. And all the sons of Levi gathered them-selves together unto him. And he said unto them, Thus saith the LORD God of Israel, Put every man his sword by his side, and go in and out from gate to gate throughout the camp, and slay every man his brother, and every man his companion, and every man his neighbour. And the children of Levi did according to the word of Moses: and there fell of the people that day about three thou-sand men"

Exodus 32: 19 - 28

Earlier, Moses was also angered by Pharaoh's hard-ened heart and his refusal to listen to God and to let the Israelites go (Exodus 11:8). You likewise have a right to have a godly anger to bring about change, godliness and justice in the society.

These scenarios confirm that when your godliness is insulted, it will surely result in anger. However, this is a godly anger which is needed in the society today just like in the time of Moses. Therefore, if men and women stand up against every form of ungodliness and injustice in the society and in the nation, people will know and embrace the truth, godliness and development. In the long run, the people will be better for it.

"Injustice anywhere is a threat to justice everywhere" (Dr Martin Luther King Jr.)

To some extent, it is almost blasphemous to think that insult, anger and irritation could be a positive force. Yet, history has taught us that the different sentiments, feelings and reactions we sometimes have could be used to achieve the best results.

Our passion, even our insult, could be turned into a blessing. Our anger could become a force of deliverance. In most cases, people who don't feel insulted by the ungodliness and injustice around them do not do anything about it.

It is those people who feel insulted and angered by the injustice around them end up doing something about it. Those people who don't feel that kind of sentiment, insult and anger become complacent, indifferent and sometimes aloof from the realities of their days.

How then do individuals who do not feel insulted or does not have holy anger be insulted by vices in the society, such as injustice, ungodliness, oppression and other kinds of crime against humanity. What is the reason for anyone not to feel insulted by such injustice in the society? It is either these kinds of people are benefiting from the system or they are ignorant of the right thing, or probably they have lost hope in themselves or society.

However, there is no other time than now for a clarion call against every apparatus of injustice in our society. That is, a call to be insulted by injustice, a desire to do something about it, and to bring about a change, no matter how little the change could be and is something that is worth standing for. This call is neither a call to carry a placard or a gun, but it is a call to stand up for what is right and just in society.

If I may ask you, at what point or level is a person, a community or a nation insulted by injustice? At the point I call the 'melting point', that is when things are no longer the same. When things are no longer the same for whom? This is when it is no longer the same in the mind of the oppressed, for the insulted person, for the community and for the nation.

'THE CHANGE NEEDED'

Rosa Parks was an example of someone who was insulted by injustice. This was when she refused to stand up or give up her seat for a white passenger in 1955. On 1 December 1955, during a typical evening rush-hour in Montgomery, Alabama, the 42-year-old woman took a seat on the bus on her way home from the Montgomery Fair department store where she worked as a seamstress. This occurrence was not the first experience for her; however, she refused to give up her seat on this occasion. Therefore, in 'holy anger', she refused to let it be business as usual.

Maybe you have a passion to see justice and godliness

in the society. Maybe you need to lead a 'godly revolution' to bring about change in your community. Remember, heaven will always support your godly move; be it a righteous cause or be it a desire to see people free from what has held them down. Perhaps, you may be the Moses your generation have been waiting for.

What could make people to stand and endure injustice, to bend and endure injustice, or to crawl and endure injustice? It is because they do not feel insulted by it. It is because they do not have any anger towards such.

> *"So that they caused the cry of the poor to come unto him, and he heareth the cry of the afflicted. When he giveth quietness, who then can make trouble? And when he hideth his face, who then can behold him? Whether it be done against a nation, or against a man only. That the hypocrite reign not, lest the people be ensnared"*
>
> *Job 34:28 – 30*

The above Scripture unveils some truth:
- That the wicked causes the poor and the afflicted to cry unto the Lord, and He hears their cry.
- That God can make a person, a city or a nation to experience quietness or trouble.
- That both a person and a nation can experience God's presence, peace or not having access to Him.
- That the purpose of all of these is that the wicked do not come to power, so that the people are not ensnared.

Therefore, it is the people who are afflicted with ungodliness and injustice that would cry unto the Lord for change. God is reciprocally responding to the cry of the afflicted. It is evident that the afflicted are basically the majority or only set of people who are insulted by injustice in society today. However, a cry, a decision and an action will bring about the change needed.

AFFLICTION AND INJUSTICE

The main recipients of injustice in any society are the afflicted, the distressed and the troubled one, both in soul and in body. Indeed, a troubled soul is a troubled life. That is, they are the set of people that are daily insulted, afflicted, denied needed necessity, denied having their voices to be heard, denied an assurance and hope for a future.

"And he spake a parable unto them to this end, that men ought always to pray, and not to faint; Saying, There was in a city a judge, which feared not God, neither regarded man: And there was a widow in that city; and she came unto him, saying, Avenge me of mine adversary. And he would not for a while: but afterward he said within himself, Though I fear not God, nor regard man; Yet because this widow troubleth me, I will avenge her, lest by her continual coming she weary me. And the Lord said, Hear what the unjust judge saith"

Luke 18: 1 - 6

The widow in the above passage kept going to the wicked judge in expectation of justice for herself. She refused to give up and become weary, and instead, the unjust and the ungodly judge himself became weary. Just as we saw in the earlier story of Malala; she refused to give up or to be diverted from the path she had chosen.

The story of the widow revealed how not to turn away from believing in justice and godliness. This widow had been insulted and afflicted with injustice, and she decided to stand up to humbly ask and demand justice for herself. She refused to give up; she refused to walk away from her desire and her godly right. In your quest for justice, an indication you have been insulted by injustice, you must never consider giving up or walk away from demanding justice.

THE COMPANY OF THE INSULTED

Recently, there seems to be an increasing number of people standing up to demand for one thing or another. Such groups include 'the black lives matter group' and 'bring back our girls'. Indeed, anyone with a just cause must voice out and be joined to a company that will see to it that justice, light and righteousness have their rightful place in the land.

> *"David therefore departed thence, and escaped to the cave Adullam: and when his brethren and all his father's house heard it, they went down thither to him. And every one that was in distress, and every one that was in debt, and every one that was discontented gathered themselves unto him; and he became a captain over them: and there were with him about four hundred men"*
>
> *1 Samuel 22:1-2*

Those that were in distress, those that were in debt

and those that were discontented with the status quo joined themselves unto David. What was the reason that necessitated this move? First of all, all these groups of people were insulted by one of these three: distress, debt and discontentment.

"Then there was a famine in the days of David three years, year after year; and David enquired of the LORD. And the LORD answered, it is for Saul, and for his bloody house, because he slew the Gibeonites"

1 Samuel 21: 1

This was an example of the atrocities of King Saul during his reign. Many therefore were willing to leave the city if it could save them from his 'madness'. Among them were these sets of individuals who were fed up with the status quo.

"Now these are they that came to David to Ziklag, while he yet kept himself close because of Saul the son of Kish: and they were among the mighty men, helpers of the war. They were armed with bows, and could use both the right hand and the left in hurling stones and shooting arrows out of a bow, even of Saul's brethren of Benjamin"

1 Chronicle 12: 1 – 2

People kept coming to David to escape from Saul just as David himself escaped. They found solace and help from being with him and they were of help to him also. These were the men who later became the mighty men of war. For any display of displeasure or anger against injustice and ungodliness, there is a reward and a godly result.

These were individuals who were distressed as a result of corruption in the land caused by ungodliness, injustice and the competitive jealousy of King Saul. Who were these people?

- These were individuals who were in debts as a result of bad management, bad policies and bad leadership of those appointed to the throne like King Saul.

- These were individuals who were discontented with the status quo and who were angry with the situation around them. This is the reason why they ran to David and found comfort in him.

However, a lot of people are in distress today and they refuse to seek help. We see a common thing in all of these men; they have all been insulted by injustice. Just as we mentioned earlier, they have been insulted by the ungodliness, injustice and wickedness of King Saul. At the end of being with David, be it for months or for years, all of these men eventually became great men in their own rank.

This was because their lives were transformed as a result of having been with David, who coached and instructed them well. David made something great out of each and everyone of them. They became enlightened, encouraged and useful for themselves and became part of David's army.

David, who was already insulted by the ungodliness and persecution of Saul's 'madness', encouraged himself in the Lord. Likewise, David turned these individuals into an army of strong men, who refused to give up but stood with him to the end. For every seed of godliness, kindness and justice sowed, there will be surely be a harvest of goodness, significance and greatness as it was with these men who came to David.

Perhaps you may need to look for a mentor or a coach to help you stand against the injustice you are facing. Take a step towards actualizing the very thing you are persuaded for and do not allow injustice to silence your voice.

Eventually, David now became a rallying point for everyone that has been insulted by injustice and tyranny under the rulership of King Saul. All of a sudden, David had raised a company of the insulted; the distressed, those in debt and the discontented people who had turned their lives around for good.

THE UNGODLY RULER AND INJUSTICE

"And Saul spake to Jonathan his son, and to all his servants, that they should kill David. But Jonathan, Saul's son, delighted much in David: and Jonathan told David, saying, Saul my father seeketh to kill thee: now therefore, I pray thee, take heed to thyself until the morning, and abide in a secret place, and hide thyself"

1 Samuel 19: 1, 2

When a hypocrite or a wicked leader is in power, anyone that becomes popular or stands out easily becomes a prey. Such individuals are subjected to bondage and witchcraft in the hand of such an ungodly leader. In such a city, nation or society, the people are given no voice.

That was the case of King Saul when he began to turn against the people he was chosen to protect and began killing the priests of God. For example, a whole company of the priests and generations of priests were slaughtered by King Saul.

It is those that are insulted by injustice that will refuse to be silenced. They will simply cry out and be heard no matter how long it takes and no matter the danger involved.

Another example was the story of the widow and the unjust judge, which we mentioned earlier, as recorded in the book of Luke 18. She refused to be quiet even in the face of shame and ridicule. She was persistent until she got what she was looking for.

A recent example is that of Malala, as mentioned in the introduction of this book. This girl refused to be silenced even in the face of threat and great danger. These people have become an example for those that are being insulted by injustice and cruelty.

Just as these people refused to give up, so likewise you must refuse to succumb to every ungodliness and injustice. Be prepared therefore to stand against every form of injustice and ungodliness around you.

COMMON INJUSTICE IN THE SOCIETY

From generation to generation, there seems to be some common occurrences. Some of the common occurrences of injustice are the presence of poverty, starvation, gender inequality, neglected widows and orphans and the injustice towards other vulnerable groups of people.

The 'Boko Haram' group were totally against western education and have been waging war against the innocent. Gender inequality is what Malala has been speaking about and protesting against. A group of people decided to fight against the education of the female children. They see or perceive the education of a female child as a threat to them. However, someone like Malala see it as being insulted by injustice, which is a crime against humanity. She also saw it as a slap and an assault on their God-given right, an opportunity to develop themselves even as male children are given the opportunity to do.

The human voice is still the most paramount vessel or weapon to use, to uphold justice and to protest against injustice. A voice of one insulted by injustice will make others to be delivered from the same injustice. My friend, your strength and your power also lies in your voice. Choose to make your voice to be heard loud and clear. It's been said that "a closed mouth is a closed destiny".

"A closed mouth is a closed destiny"
(Bishop David Oyedepo)

The following story will throw more light on the above quote.

It is the story of Jabez whose mother named him 'child of sorrow'. In other words, his name was synonymous to sorrow. This story reflects the injustice in the home which is the first foundation of any society. The greatest injustice anyone could do to an innocent baby, coming into this world to fulfil a latent glorious destiny, is to place an embargo of evil on that child. Unfortunately, his mother placed such an embargo upon a glorious destiny by naming him 'child of sorrow'.

It came to the consciousness of Jabez to call on a higher power that could set him free. In other words, he re-fused to be silent. Imagine if Jabez had been silent and received such a seal which heaven had never authorised, he would have lived and died that way. Indeed, a closed mouth is a closed destiny.

> *"And Jabez was more honourable than his breth-ren: and his mother called his name Jabez, say-ing, Because I bare him with sorrow. And Jabez called on the God of Israel, saying, Oh that thou wouldest bless me indeed, and enlarge my coast, and that thine hand might be with me, and that thou wouldest keep me from evil, that it may not grieve me! And God granted him that which he requested"*
>
> *1 Chronicle 4: 9, 10*

The prayer of Jabez to the God of all flesh was a divine door opened to him and a turnaround for his life; from sorrow to celebration. He became an honourable man because he refused to be quiet.

The second story speaks of injustice from the com-munity.

There was a man named Bartimaeus. He was blind for most of his life as we were not told how long he had been in that condition. However, one could imagine that he had been on that particular junction for most of his life, asking for alms.

However, on a certain day, the Lord Jesus was passing by the junction of the street where blind Bartimeus had been sitting for years. Just as he heard the movement of the crowd, he was able to confirm what was going, and he was told that Jesus of Nazareth, the Healer, was passing by.

All of a sudden, this blind man saw this as a lifetime opportunity for him to regain his sight. So he did something unusual; he began to shout at the top of his voice; "Jesus, Son of David, have mercy on me". However, the community - the people close to him that could have helped him - did him a great deal of injustice. They actually told him to shut up and be silent.

His eyes were already closed and they also wanted him likewise to close his mouth. That was a great injustice. However, he refused to be silent. The Lord Jesus then called him and he miraculously regained his sight. This was because he refused to be silent. A sealed mouth indeed is a sealed destiny.

In other words, voicing out against injustice in the society is championing a just cause. You can stand for a just cause; voice out and stand against injustice. I could say; 'mother' of injustice is a closed mouth. Poverty is possible in every society because someone refused to speak out. Imagine a life without an opportunity to speak; imagine everyone communicating only with hands or with eyes, perhaps no one might have been able to speak against injustice in the society.

HUMAN CAPABILITY AND INJUSTICE

There is a level of positive anger that needed to be alive and to make a head way in this life. Without this measure of anger against injustice, a person, a society or a whole nation would have to live perpetually under the bondage of injustice.

That was the kind of anger displayed by Malala in Pakistan against the embargo of the Taliban towards the education of females. Malala's anger made her to defy the Taliban's threat and possible death. That's the kind of anger that every member of society, every citizen of a nation must possess if they have ever been insulted by injustice.

Do not die in silence, do not wallow in shame - you no longer have to endure being insulted by ungodliness. Your soul is crying, so give your soul a chance to voice out before it is too late. There is an innate and strong desire in every human being to be heard. Make sure you speak out and loud enough to be heard.

INJUSTICE IN THE NEIGHBOURHOOD

You have heard or witnessed different instances of injustice around you, in your community, in your nation and in the global society at large.

For example, one fateful day on 9 August 2014, a young promising youth by name Michael Brown was fatally shot by a white police officer by the name Darren Wilson, in the town of Fergusson, Missouri, in the United States. Since that moment and from that town, the campaign of 'black lives matter' has been spreading to every part of the country.

Looking back, we can ask and examine if there has even been any positive outcome or results from this campaign. Moreover, this campaign has not only been among the African-American, but even being supported by the white people and the Latinos.

Definitely, the campaign or the peaceful protests have yielded some positive results. First, I am a not a judge and do not try to portray myself as one, but this group of people have been surely insulted by so much injustice, even for centuries.

These people have been able to speak out and there are a few positive results that can be seen already:

- putting a check on the police officers. Presently, cameras are being used to monitor what goes on when they are in contact with potential offenders or suspects.

- political office holders are already looking into how there can be better policing in the society.

- bringing better opportunities to African-American societies in different parts of the nation.

- this has also enabled African-Americans to be able to speak out with one voice at such a time as this.

Such positive results are another proof to confirming the importance of not keeping silent in the face of injustice and ungodliness. Whether it is found on the street, in the community or where you least expect it, it is important and paramount to eliminate ungodliness and injustice. A sincere decision to make is to refuse to give up until the society experiences the defeat of every form of injustice and ungodliness.

When insulted by injustice, face it, stand up against it and demand your right and justice. Keep hope alive because as you do and do not give up, you will surely be rewarded for every seed of good deed and godliness.

Your voice may not be loud today or be heard today, but make sure you are still standing on your feet. That is, if your voice is not heard, let your head be seen. Moreover, make sure you are standing for something you believe in. Keep speaking; speak hope to yourself, speak out your opinion too. You never know, you may be the change and light needed by others, to shine on their path. You can become a shining light for others.

This would be a reality because you have decided to live a transformed life and have allowed yourself to be a pedestal that brings transformation to others who are being insulted by injustice daily in the society.

This is the way to shine; to make a difference even as you choose to stand up, speak out and maintain a valid positive opinion. Therefore, guard yourself with a positive attitude, conviction, hope and fulfilment of your heart's desire. Such social justice could be at the corner not only for you but for others.

ORDINANCES OF JUSTICE

"Cry aloud, spare not, lift up thy voice like a trumpet, and shew my people their transgression, and the house of Jacob their sins. Yet they seek me daily, and delight to know my ways, as a nation that did righteousness, and forsook not the ordinance of their God: they ask of me the ordinances of justice; they take delight in approaching to God"

Isaiah 58:2b

The scenario portrayed in the passage above speaks of hypocritical lifestyles that human beings outside of God could be living in. This happens when individuals merely speak on how they seek God but their hearts are far from Him. The ways and statutes of God refer to His ordinance, His laws and His commandments.

Naturally, ordinance means an authoritative rule or law; a decree or a command. There is a command from the Creator Himself on how His creations should relate to one another, justly or unjustly. God's ordinances have therefore been given and it is expected for man to find out how to live his life and relate to others in society. This is where you find justice and godliness and knowledge to fight every form of ungodliness and injustice.

"How long will you judge unjustly, and accept the persons of the wicked? Defend the poor and fatherless,: do justice to the afflicted and needy"

Psalm 82:3

You remember the story of the widow and the unjust judge? Yes, some people are more susceptible to injustice than others, people like the widows, the fatherless or motherless, the poor and the afflicted inclusive. Who will stand for them, who will speak for them, who will defend them? It could be me or you.

"Injustice anywhere is a threat to justice everywhere" (Dr Martin Luther Jnr.)

Therefore, be ready to stand for someone, choose to speak for someone, and be a defence for someone. Choose to do these especially for those susceptible to injustice and ungodliness, such as the widows, the fatherless, the motherless, the poor and the afflicted. I can assure you these have a long-lasting and fulfilling reward.

"He will give justice to the poor and make a fair decision for the exploited..."

Isaiah 11:4 (NLT)

The Lord is concerned about the poor receiving justice and that they are not neglected or cheated.

"Thus says the LORD, keep judgement, and do justice... Blessed is the man that does this, and the son of man that lays hold on it"

Isaiah 56: 1a, 2

There is a commanded blessing on anyone that values, esteems and stands for justice in society. Those who have been insulted by ungodliness and injustice could be in a good or better position to stand for or with those that are being insulted by the same.

Therefore, in the struggle possessing godly anger and campaigning against injustice in the land, everyone in this 'ship' must stay together. In this way, you become eyes for one another, you become hands for one another, you become feet for one another and you become voices for one another. With these in place, the joint campaign against injustice shall be successful.

ADVOCACY

In Nigeria, the Ogoni struggle and campaign for justice has been for decades during which individuals fighting for justice have been jailed and killed. Those days were simply dark days for the people and the nation in general. This was because the people were demanding social justice as a result of the natural resources found on their land.

It's either the people were not benefiting from the resources or the people were being molested and their land, their farm produce and source of livelihood were been destroyed as a result of the misuse of those God-given resources. All these troubles were confronting the people.

One day, an advocate for justice gathered around sixteen thousand farmers and fisher men. These were people who had their farms and river damaged due to oil leakages between 2008 and 2009. He stood with them and became their voices before the court of law. That was when they were able to get reasonable justice.

In Kenya, the Mau Mau Uprising, also known as the 'Mau Mau Revolt', the 'Mau Mau Rebellion' or 'Kenya Emergency', was a military conflict that took place in Kenya between 1952 and 1960. It involved Kikuyu-dominated groups summarily called Mau Mau.

The 'mau mau' rebellion that had people tortured by foreign power was able to receive justice after a long time of waiting. Insult by injustice will always be dealt with which is going to be with one voice and with one purpose. This is the reason why you must keep making sure your voice is heard for every right cause.

In Congo, it has been reported that there is no chance of any justice at all. This kind of situation could be due to a long time of injustice, resilience of the people and corruption or all of the above.

Today, one can have hope that ungodliness and injustice will not be an ongoing thing. There is still hope that if the people refuse to give up and keep silent, no matter how long or inconsequential their voices could be at the beginning, it would still be heard and justice be served.

This is the call; to keep dreaming, to keep praying and hoping and to stand up for what it's worth living for. This is the way and manner to stand against injustice of all kinds. This is the way to make your life count, to make a difference and shine forth in the world full of darkness.

CHAPTER TWO

POWER OF PARLIAMENT AND PEN

POWER OF PARLIAMENT AND PEN

Parliament is made up of people voted to make laws. Laws are made for the people. The people are not made for the law. Therefore, the law or any practice that is not for the good of the people must be changed.

William Wilberforce used his presence in the English Parliament to bring a change to a practice that was dehumanizing – the slave trade. This informs us that Wilberforce was angry at something and it was the ungodliness that was taking place in his time.

In this chapter, we will look at his life and other individuals who have become examples for us today. Who were they? They were people who were simply angry and furious by the ungodliness in their time. Likewise, they have acted promptly, properly and accordingly; they made use of the platform and power they had to bring about change.

Taking a quote from Edward I. Wheeler, who said; "The pen is mightier than the sword".

"The pen is mightier than the sword"
(Edward I. Wheeler)

We will now look at an example in the Bible of a 'senior parliamentarian'; Joseph, a Prime Minister in his rank, who through his wisdom brought change to

Egypt under Pharaoh's authority. Also, through his God-given wisdom he made history in Egypt and the nations around.

> **"He made him lord of his house, and ruler of all his substance: To bind his princes at his pleasure; and teach his senators wisdom"**
>
> *Psalm 105: 21, 22.*

This chapter deals with people, who through their position as a Parliamentarian and those who through their pens, brought great change to the people. This is because they felt insulted by the ungodliness around them. Every society is run by the law and regulations made by the Parliament of that nation. Moreover, it takes wisdom, power and influence to be able to make a positive impact on what goes on in society and in the nation as a whole.

Wisdom for what? Wisdom to institute laws and regulations, which enables the people, insulted by ungodliness, to have the right, the choice and the opportunity to voice out and stand out against every ungodliness, nefarious and injustice in the society. In every civilized society, there is an established institution put in place to design laws that make people live civilized and having rights and privileges as citizens of that nation.

These individuals are people we will discuss in this chapter. We will look into their lives and elucidate how their anger brought about the needed change in the land. It is a privilege to learn and emulate such individuals.

WILLIAM WILBERFORCE AND ABOLITION
OF THE SLAVE TRADE

William Wilberforce was a man who lived between 1759 and 1833. He was elected into the House of Commons in England at the age of 21. He had an idea, an understanding and a conviction, that all men are born equal. A belief that no one should be a slave to his fellow human; that everyone has a right to life and freedom to live where he or she chooses.

Slave trade in the 18th and 19th century was a booming business to many influential people. However, at best, it is degrading and insulting to human beings, created in the image and likeness of God. This is one of the ungodliness of men that humanity at that time was insulted by. This is the battle William Wilberforce spent his entire life fighting because he felt insulted by the ungodliness of the slave trade.

The platform of Parliament was a good and needed one for Wilberforce to exercise his God-given vision and passion which was to see the end of slavery in his day. If it is at Parliament that laws are made, then there is a need for a law that will terminate this practice of ungodliness, called slave trade. This was the destiny of Wilberforce.

This suggests to me that there are people that are to champion the campaign and advocacy against the cycle of ungodliness and injustice in every nation. This was the experience of Wilberforce and likewise you need to stand up and live for what will bring justice and liberation to humanity.

WILBERFORCE AND HIS RESPONSIBILITIES

Wilberforce saw himself as a man with a great responsibility for the good of mankind. He was convinced that this opportunity was born out of the love of Christ. He was convinced that Membership of Parliament was as a result of the God-given responsibilities to set humanity free from slavery.

> *"My business is in the world and I must mix in the assemblies of men or quit the post which Providence seems to have assigned me."*
> *(William Wilberforce)*

The above quote was a result of his conviction of his role in the assembly of men, in order to carry out the role assigned to him from Heaven.

> *"Great indeed are our opportunities; great also is our responsibility"*
> *(William Wilberforce)*

This is part of his quotes reflecting his belief that the more your opportunities are in life, the more will be your responsibilities. So, I challenge you my friend, please never misuse your God-given opportunities, it may be the path to fulfilling your destiny.

WILLIAM WILBERFORCE THE WRITER

The power of the pen for Wilberforce was an additional weapon as it were, added to his membership of the

Parliament of England. He did not only lift his voice as a formidable weapon in Parliament, he also lifted his pen as a weapon too. His pen moved freely on the canvas for all to read and be inspired.

Wilberforce used his writings to promote the cause of justice in his generation and beyond. He lived freely, yet his soul was in bondage with those in slavery; those insulted by ungodliness and injustice. It was the love of Christ, according to him, that enabled and strengthened him to do all that he was able to do.

"No one expects to attain to the height of learning, or arts, or power, or wealth, or military glory, without vigorous resolution, strenuous diligence, and steady perseverance. Yet we expect to be Christians without labour, study, or inquiry" (William Wilberforce)

The above quote is part of the writings of Wilberforce, a man who put ink on the canvass and paper, in order to promote his beliefs, philosophy and his campaign for the abolition of the slave trade. His writings were basically centred on his belief in His Lord and his love for Him.

Wilberforce spent a good time spreading his campaign to end the slave trade through his writings. This is to tell you the effect, the impact and power of the pen in standing against injustice.

Through his quotes, Wilberforce saw inconvenient situations, strenuous and laborious situations as part of the ingredients needed to fulfil a just cause. So Wilberforce counted all his labour towards the abolition of slave trade as necessary. As it is said; 'nothing good comes easy'. If you are going to speak out against injustice, if you are angry at ungodliness in the society, then you have the opposing force to contend against.

It is my sincere opinion that Wilberforce might have been faced with an opposing force in his day; he was well equipped with a greater force working for him. Therefore, your insult by the ungodliness and injustice in the land is a force. Like Wilberforce did, you must build and develop a greater force on the inside of you. In this way, you will be able to speak and stand against ungodliness and injustice in the land.

One of the forces that Wilberforce engaged in was his pen on the canvass. Not only that, he was also writing on the canvass of the mind of people. The writings of Wilberforce remain an enigma and his coming to Parliament was just for one cause; for the abolition of the slave trade. In the latter path of his life, when he resigned from Parliament due to his health, his mind and soul was still engaged in Parliament, especially as it related to his Bill on the abolition of the slave trade.

It is therefore not surprising that some days after the Bill was passed, he slept in his Lord. Wilberforce could as well be referred to as a lawmaker appointed by the Lord, to make godly laws for Him. Just as his voice could not be silenced at Parliament, likewise, his pen was doing mightily to set a deprived and helpless people free.

THE LAWMAKERS AND THE DIRECTIONS OF NATIONS

William Wilberforce was an example of the role a lawmaker could play in the development of a nation. The good news is that this man of great purpose and significance, who impacted his generation and the generations thereafter, was a believer in Christ Jesus. If lawmakers in nations today refused to be bribed and be corrupted by some larger-than-life leaders, the people will be less insulted and molested by ungodliness and injustice. God is therefore looking for lawmakers today, who will make godly laws, just as He raised lawgivers in the generations past.

"Gilead is mine, and Manasseh is mine; Ephraim also is the strength of mine head; Judah is my lawgiver"

Psalm 60:7

God has individuals He has positioned for His purpose and to be used as His vessel at different time and season. However, these people are not just going to be found only on the crusade platform or on the church pulpit alone, but in different spheres of life.

They are going to be found in politics, Wall Street, in the Arts, in Hollywood, in the Media, Sports, Music and Technology and so on. These are those who are going to be used of Him to speak out, to stand up and to render assistance to all that are insulted by ungodliness, insulted and molested by injustice. These are those who are going to be role models to others, in the campaign against ungodliness and injustice that is permeating the nations of the 21st century.

Actually, everyone, in one way or the other is being insulted by ungodliness and injustice, be it racial injustice, inequality, economical injustice, and the spread and campaign of ungodliness sweeping the land. What matters now is how prepared are you to surmount these mountains that are confronting the society. Now is the time to act!

THE LAWMAKER, THE NATION
AND HER DIRECTION

"The princes digged the well, the nobles of the people digged it, by the direction of the lawgiver..."

Numbers 21:18

The direction to go as seen in the above Scriptures was given by the lawgiver. They definitely must be patriotic and have a good heart towards the people they are leading. These lawgivers or lawmakers are people with the interest of the people at heart, to see each one freed from ungodliness and injustice.

Indeed, each and everyone given as examples above - in politics, media, music industry, etc, are all 'lawmakers' in their own rights. That is, they are in one way or another impacting their generation with what comes out of them, which is what the people will likely follow. It is time therefore that each one speaks out; be angry, I challenge you, at the ungodliness and injustice that you see around you.

You are a lawmaker in your own right. Whenever you are being insulted by ungodliness and injustice, endeavour to speak against it, endeavour to stand up against it, and expect to see change. This is acting as a 'lawmaker'; not just insulted or molested by ungodliness and injustice, but confronting it; speak against ungodliness before the earth and in the place of prayer before Heavenly Throne.

THE WILLING LEADERS

"My heart is toward the governor of Israel, that offered themselves willingly among the people. Bless ye the LORD. Speak, ye that ride on white asses, ye that sit in judgement, and walk by the way. They that are delivered from the noise of the archers in the place of drawing of water ..."

Judges 5: 9-11a.

Again, an example of a willing leader was William Wilberforce who jettisoned his prestigious position as a Member of Parliament in the United Kingdom for a vision and passion he felt was more important.

However, he was advised by a Minister of the gospel that, that would not be right but to still use the same platform of being a member of the parliament to fight against the slave trade.

Wilberforce wanted to forego Parliament because of his passion to see the abolition of slave trade; he was simply angry at ungodliness and injustice around him. Thank God, he was rightly counselled not to leave Parliament. That tells you and me that Wilberforce was willing to fulfil his vision; willing to pay any logical, civilized and moral price, in order to speak, write and fight against ungodliness and injustice that was insulting him. You too can ask yourself, what price am I willing to pay in order to speak and to stand up against ungodliness and injustice?

From the above Scripture, the governor, the judges and the lawmakers of Israel were willing to serve their people. They were willing to bring justice to all, willing to deliver their people from terrorism and the slave traders of their generation. They were willing to stand against child trafficking and not just to talk about it. They were willing to give justice and equality to all. Are you ready to be part of this movement?

LAWMAKERS COMMAND OBEDIENCE

"The sceptre shall not depart from Judah, nor a lawgiver from between his feet, until Shiloh come; and unto him shall the gathering of the people be"

Genesis 49:10

The people that you see in Parliament all over the world are the symbol of authority given to the lawmakers to make laws. Lawmakers therefore command authority in the way the people are governed. From the above Scripture, another version says; *"... unto him shall the obedience of the people be"*.

In other words, the lawmakers possess the authority that commands the obedience of the people. That is, each law that is passed is to be obeyed by the people. Therefore, every lawmaker is expected to feel insulted by ungodliness and injustice, in order to be able to make laws that will bring justice, freedom and equity for the people.

In your own right, wherever you may be, you are influencing someone; so endeavour to make 'laws' that will impart others rightly. Definitely not a law that will make them to be insulted the more by ungodliness and injustice. This is the clarion call; this is the exemplary life Wilberforce had lived and is expected to be emulated for the love of the people and the nation.

ABRAHAM AND THE PARLIAMENT
OF HEAVEN

Almost every human being on earth believes that 'heaven's constitutions' rules the earth. Moreover, every human being and every animal recognizes that, heaven's ordinance rules the earth. The Creator of heaven and earth made all visible and invisible things and all are subject to His order. Everything He has created are under His control, both living and non-living, and all are subject to His laws, including the sun, the moon, the stars, the eagle, the dolphin, the gorilla and every human being.

This is what I call the Parliament of Heaven, which governs and controls what happens and when it happens. There was a person who was invited into this 'Heaven's Parliament', his name was Abraham. He was invited to participate in a deliberation which will determined the destiny of a city and thousands of its inhabitants.

"And the LORD said, shall I hide from Abraham that thing which I do; Seeing that Abraham shall surely become a great and mighty nation, and all the nations of the earth shall be blessed in him? For I know him, that he will command his children and his household after him, and they shall keep the way of the LORD, to do justice and judgement; that the LORD may upon Abraham that which He has spoken of him. That be far from thee to do after this manner, to slay the righteous with the wicked, to slay the righteous with the wicked: and that the righteous should be as the wicked; that be far from thee: Shall not the Judge of the earth

do right? And he said, Behold now, I have taken upon me to speak unto the Lord:"

Genesis 18: 17-19, 25,31a

Abraham was informed about the judgement that was coming upon Sodom. What was the reason why the God of heaven and earth informed Abraham His friend about the decision on Sodom? The reasons were:

- Abraham was His covenant man on earth and He would like him to participate in this scenario.

- Because all the nations of the earth will be blessed through Abraham. Therefore, Abraham as a man of influence in all the nations of the earth was representing all the nations. This was the first meeting between heaven and Abraham, the representative of the nations.

- Abraham was going to raise children who will operate by justice on the earth and was therefore setting a legacy for all the nations of the earth.

Therefore, all the nations will learn justice through the offspring of Abraham, this then would become a legacy for all to learn and emulate from. With this participation of Abraham in this forum, he humbly accepted his role as God's anchorman to establish justice on earth among other things. Abraham took it upon himself to speak and to intercede for the city in the presence of the LORD.

This scenario further shows the God of heaven and earth as a just and righteous God. Therefore, the foundation was laid, the legacy was confirmed that justice will always be sought and established on earth.

Abraham started by asking for consensus from the LORD; that if 50 righteous people were found in the city of Sodom, it won't be destroyed. He then asked until he got to 10 righteous, and the LORD still gave him His words that if that was found 10, the city will not be wiped off from the earth. However, 10 righteous people were not found. In other words, Abraham asked 6 times and it was granted unto him.

This was one man standing in the position of deliberating the destiny of thousands of souls in the presence of the LORD. Abraham was given a responsibility to see to it that there is no ungodliness or injustice that should be looked away or ignored. In other words, every ungodliness and injustice must be spoken and stood against.

Abraham spoke in the presence of God for the destiny of a whole city. Abraham added his voice to what could determine the destiny of thousands of souls. He had a voice in heaven and his voice was registered on earth. Therefore, the generation of people that will judge ungodliness will see to it that justice is established on earth.

You are a part of that generation, a generation that effect God's justice on the earth. A generation that will be so much insulted by ungodliness will speak and stand against it with the strength given from Heaven. Therefore, you have received a mandate not given by man, but given and empowered by God, to bring justice to the people and godliness on the earth.

JACOB AND THE PARLIAMENT OF HEAVEN

In different parts of the world, there are different

types of Parliamentarian procedures. Likewise, there are different rules allowed in each Parliament; be it the voting rules, the nomination rules, disciplinary action, the bylaws rules and constitution amendment rules. However, there are rules that govern Heaven's parliament too.

"The secret things belong unto the LORD our God: but those things which are revealed belong unto us and to our children for ever, that we may do all the words of this law"

Deuteronomy 29: 29

The Bible passage unveils to us that there are secrets that the LORD Himself keeps, however, there are those things He chooses to share with you and I. You then need to know how to access this.

God calling a man to His Council as it were to deliberate with Him on issues or matters of destiny is something of honour. This is a demonstration that God always desire intimate fellowship with man and the children of the Kingdom. It is therefore an honour on the part of any man to be involved in what the Lord is doing

Jacob's invitation to Heaven's Parliament was somehow different from that of his grandfather Abraham. Jacob's invitation to this parliament was done because his destiny was at stake, the decision about his destiny and that of his generation was about to be made. Thus, angels were sent to him to help him through the process. Jacob was also sensitive as he knew the divine timing for himself. Notwithstanding there was danger ahead, he needed divine assistance and it was given to him. He knew his past, he knew what he did and he was afraid it could hinder his future. So, he needed the help, the assistance and transformation that can only come through the Parliament of Heaven.

> *"And Jacob went on his way, and the angels of God met him. And when Jacob saw them, he said, this is God's host: and he called the name of that place Mahanaim. And Jacob was left alone; and there wrestled a man with him until the breaking of the day. And when he saw that he prevailed not against him, he touched the hollow of his thigh; and the hollow of Jacob's thigh was out of joint, as he wrestled with him. And he said, Let me go, for the day breaketh. And he said, I will not let thee go, except thou bless me. And he said unto him, What is thy name? And he said, Jacob. And he said, Thy name shall be called no more Jacob, but Israel: for as a prince hast thou power with God and with men, and hast prevailed."*
>
> *Genesis 32: 1, 2, 24-28*

Jacob was at the transition of his life and destiny. Angels of the Lord were sent to him to assist him. This was his destiny at a crossroad; this was the birth pang of a nation about to be born. The main point of interest for you in this particular story is how Jacob was able to be adamant until he received what he desired. He was interested in protection from Esau; he was interested in the preservation of his family and future generation. Jacob seemed to be running away from his past and sometimes a man's past could haunt him.

The past of Jacob looked like this:

He cheated his brother and he refused to take responsibility; he stole someone else's identity. Maybe you have a role too and you have been running away from your role in life; be as a societal builder, nation builder or builder of the Kingdom of God.

Likewise, Jacob exhibited a lifestyle of someone who practiced ungodliness and injustice. However, what Jacob represented and sowed later sought after him. His life has been dipped into ungodliness and injustice towards others, and he surely needed divine power to make him a new person; delivered from a lifestyle of ungodliness and injustice.

Jacob being at his future father-in-law's house was cheated too. There are things that he paid for through his labour which was not given to him. It has been said that "what goes around comes around". At his father-in-law's house, Jacob was insulted by ungodliness and injustice.

Jacob therefore needed to face the ungodliness and injustice that he was battling and he needed to get some freedom from the ghost of his past. He was insulted by ungodliness in his father-in-law's house. Jacob was therefore invited to the Parliament of Heaven in order for him to have a new platform to operate from. This opportunity was offered to him to be able to negotiate his life, his way of life and for his destiny.

At last, the Angel blessed him, changed his name to Israel and declared him a prince who possessed power with God and men. Likewise, if you are going to speak and stand against ungodliness and injustice, for yourself, your family, posterity and for the society at large, you need to possess power from on high.

WILBERFORCE AND THE DIVINE SUPPORT

In the same way, William Wilberforce could not carry out what he did without the power from on high. The following letter from John Wesley, written to William Wilberforce on 24 February 1791, is evident that Wilberforce was equipped with divine power. This excerpt of the letter was culled from ChristianHistory.net.

"Unless the divine power has raised you up to be as "Athanasius against the world," I see not how you can go through your glorious enterprise in opposing that execrable villainy, which is the scandal of religion, of England, and of human nature. Unless God has raised you up for this very thing, you will be worn out by the opposition of men and devils. But if God be for you, who can be against you? Are all of them stronger than God? O be not weary of well-doing! Go on, in the name of God and in the power of His might, till even American slavery (the vilest that ever saw the sun) shall vanish away before it".

This is how to speak and stand in the presence of a daunting opposing force. Unlike Jacob, your own opposing force could be ungodliness and injustice; only make sure your voice and the power of it are not lost. The audacity of Jacob helped him and he was still able to demand what he knew was his last resort.

You as well can stand up for what you know will take you, your family, your posterity, your society and your nation to the next level. Speak against every ungodliness and injustice. Stand for the truth. In no time, you will be influencing everyone around. You will be a better person, your family will be the better people, posterity will remember you and society will be enriched, just because you were provoked.

CHAPTER THREE

FREEDOM FIGHTERS

FREEDOM FIGHTERS

According to the United Nations Charter, freedom has been declared to be the fundamental human right of everyone. To be under a physical bondage or a mental bondage is one of the worst situations someone could ever be in life. While in bondage, the strength of the mind is not put into full action in order to maximize its full potential. If a man is incarcerated physically, his soul is also incarcerated. This is because such a person might not be able to think right or think straight. Some individuals who find themselves in such situation in imprisonment, in bondage or incarceration have ended up committing suicide.

Likewise, when someone finds his or her mind is not free or in mental bondage, such a person might as well not be free physically. Freedom and right are synonyms. Therefore, if a person is not free, his right is restricted. Your right in a civilized society is to have freedom.

According to the United Nations Universal Declaration of Human Rights, Article 3 states that, "Everyone has the right to life, liberty and security of person". Therefore, someone who fights for the freedom of a people is fighting for the right of such people. This is the case of the individuals we are going to look at in this chapter. We will see their pain, their anger, their challenges, their predicaments and their power over injustice, ungodliness, demons and victories.

We are going to look at the lives of individuals who have lived exemplary lives to fight what has insulted them, such as injustice, wickedness, bondage, cruelty, corruption and wars.

This is because they saw themselves, their personalities, their beliefs and philosophies insulted by those ungodly acts.

MOSES: A MAN OF PAIN, PASSION AND POWER

"And in those days, that Moses was grown and he went out unto his brethren, and looketh on their burdens, and spied an Egyptian, smiting a man, a Hebrew, one of his brethren. And he went out on the second day, and behold two men of the Hebrews strove together: and he said to him that did the wrong, wherefore smites thou thy fellow?"

Exodus 2: 11, 13

Moses was a man who was born in the season and era of pain as a result of the bondage and slavery of his people in Egypt. Moses himself was not in bondage because he was a prince in the palace of Pharaoh. However, one way or the other, he knew that he was an Israelite, a part of those people he saw daily being mistreated and living in poverty.

Therefore, their pain was his pain too. Their bondage was his bondage, their trouble was his trouble. Moses thought that his people will realize and identify him as their deliverer. This was because he felt strongly within himself that he had an assignment to stand against the injustice, slavery and ungodly dealings through the hands of the Egyptians.

"And seeing one of them suffer wrong, he defended him, and avenged him that was oppressed, and smote the Egyptian: For he supposed his brethren would have understood how that God by his hand would deliver them: but they understood not"

Acts 7: 24, 25

This was the mindset of Moses; to demonstrate to the Israelites that he could deliver them from the terror of Pharaoh and the Egyptians. The passion of Moses took over him, the pain of Moses overwhelmed him and he thought he could deliver his people by his own power.

This is not an encouragement to take the same route that Moses took in displaying his belief, impression and passion, but let your passion be submissive to God – to His will and His direction. Let your faith be in the Lord Jesus and not in your strength, to fight against ungodliness and injustice in the society.

Moses did not intend to kill the Egyptian. However, his pain, his passion and his anger made the whole encounter lead to the death of the Egyptian. This is the extent pain and anger could lead anyone to do.

From the above story, we can see how God uses our sentiments to His own glory. Even though Moses grew up in Pharaoh's palace, he knew who he was. He could sense that the treatment of the Hebrews by the Egyptians was unfair and that irritated him. He was so angered that he eventually killed one of the abusive Egyptians.

Killed? Wow! That must be a very strong sentiment right there. I don't think too many of us are as passionate and emotional as Moses. Will God ever use him after that? Well, He did. God saw the passion and zeal in Moses and decided to redirect it for a constructive result.

Even though Moses blew it by killing that man, his passion could not be denied. What a manifestation of wisdom from God that He would actually forgive him and redirect his passion in the right direction.

"Being good is commendable, but only when it is combined with doing good is it useful"
(Anonymous)

Dear readers, can God ever use your sentiment for His own glory? What about the negative sentiments, can they ever become an instrument in the hands of the Almighty God? Can your weaknesses ever be useful to God Almighty?

Well, the story of Moses answers these questions in the affirmative. If we could be humble enough to submit our passions, sentiments and even weaknesses to God Almighty, he would successfully convert them to something positive that would eventually glorify Him.

When it comes to change; feelings like frustrations, anger and irritations can easily be converted by each person to become a powerful force of change. Basically, history tells us that the people who end up changing their world are those who had at one time or the other felt a great irritation about whatever was going on in their community at that particular time.

Moses was a freedom fighter in his own strength from the onset. He was angry at ungodliness, but no success for him until he was called in a divine manner to deliver and make freedom a reality for his own people. Moses became a great deliverer for his people because he originally felt insulted by ungodliness. This confirms the fact that, it is those that are insulted by ungodliness that makes a change in their nations. They make a difference in their generation.

HIS PASSION

Moses also had passion; passion to see change among his people. That is, he wanted to see his people completely free. What you are angry about could be what you are meant or sent to give solution to.

Moses had a passion; a compelling emotion in him which was pushing him towards his people and to be a deliverer for them. Though Moses initially missed it, he was still used of the Lord to rescue His people. This was not until when he had learned how to channel his anger and passion rightly. God was able to make use of his anger and passion when he was now able to see through the eyes of God.

Moses went through the process; he went through the breaking and came out as a new man. If you want to make impact and a difference, it is obvious you cannot do it in your strength or power.

> *"By faith Moses, when he was come to years, refused to be called the son of Pharaoh's daughter; Choosing rather to suffer affliction with the people of God, than to enjoy the pleasures of sins for a season;"*
>
> *Hebrews 11: 24, 25*

His passion would not allow him to be referred to as a grandson of Pharaoh, perhaps an heir to the throne. There was a passion in him that was bigger, better and greater to him than being a prince in Egypt. There was a destiny in him which was crying, and that which he recognized was to bring freedom to his people. This destiny started as a passion and as a result of this, he suffered affliction from Pharaoh who saw his style and the direction he was going as hostile to him and his kingdom.

What are you having a strong passion for? Is it a passion that is people-oriented, can it impact lives, would people be better for it and does it glorify God? Then, I can tell you and convince you that you should consider going for it.

HIS POWER

Moses was a prince and was born with a measure of power. However, he seemed to be interested only in his true destiny; the destiny of being a deliverer and freedom fighter for his people. He has been fighting with his fist up until now, but he definitely needed a greater strength and power for him to be able to fulfil and accomplish that destiny of been a deliverer and a freedom fighter for his people.

> *"And seeing one of them suffer wrong, he defended him, and avenged him that was oppressed, and smote the Egyptian: For he supposed his brethren would have understood how that God by his hands would deliver them: but they understood not. This Moses whom they refused, saying, who made thee a ruler and a judge? The same did God send to be a ruler and a deliverer ..."*
>
> *Acts 7: 24, 25, 35*

He was initially using human strength, but the assignment stirring on the inside of him, was bigger than that of the strength and wisdom of Egypt. He surely needed a power that was not of the flesh or of his own making; he later discovered that he needed the divine power of God. That was what the job and the assignment required.

Where he had being rejected and despised before, he was now accepted and honoured. This was because he has received divine power. He was now their deliverer. The past was gone and a new day began.

Definitely, if Moses did not have the passion right from the beginning to be the freedom fighter or to be the deliverer for his people, it may be that he might not have been able to do what he did as a deliverer of the Israelites. Perhaps, if he had allowed the hurts and humiliation of the past to hinder or debar him, he might not have been able to be the deliverer of his people. This was because his heart had to be in what he was destined to do as a freedom fighter or as a deliverer.

Likewise, you must not allow the hurt of the past to haunt or hinder you from fulfilling and performing your duties as one who has a passion to impact his society and make a change. You also will pay one price or the other for the assignment you are meant to perform. Only discover it and go for it. Don't lose sight of it, but go for it, be a deliverer of people from ungodliness, injustice and other crimes against humanity. That is where your passion would find fulfilment.

MARTIN LUTHER KING JNR.

The history of the civil right in the United States will not be completed without mentioning the effort and solidifying impact of Rev. Dr Martin Luther King Jnr. Dr. King's life on earth was a very short one, but the impact of his life is still being felt by hundreds of millions to say the least. He was born on 15 January 1929 and was assassinated on 4 April 1968.

He was a Baptist Minister who took over the preaching after his father. However, his impact was very much felt as a civil rights activist. That was his destiny; he only used the pulpit to spread his message. That message focussed on speaking against segregation and the dehumanizing attitude towards black people and how they were being placed in social and mental bondage even after slavery had officially ended.

HIS PASSION

Dr. King's passion was born out of his desire to see all people including the African-American live and co-exist side by side, in line with the creed of the founding fathers, that all men are born equal. He had a good education, was brilliant and had good opportunities, but he was aware of millions of others who were living in poverty and with no dignity or human rights.

One of Dr. King's statements was "The greatness of America lies in the right to protest for right".

"The greatness of America lies in the right to protest for right" (Martin Luther King Jnr.)

Dr. King was furious at injustice and ungodliness, insincerity and the dehumanizing experience the African-American people were subjected to, just because of the color of their skin. These were what brought about the passion of Dr Martin Luther King. He lived a short but extraordinary life that impacted not only his generation but many generations after him. He was able to use the pulpit as a platform for freedom fighting. His life in a way can be compared to that of Moses who grew up in the palace and never allowed the affluence of the palace to blindfold him from following his destiny.

Likewise, Dr. King was exposed to a good life compared to millions of others who were with little or no privileges. Dr. King jumped two specific grades while in high school because of his excellent performance. He attended college at a tender age of 15. Even today in the United States, there are so many teens that are not opportune to have such privileges that Dr. King enjoyed in his days as a student. That however, was not an excuse for him to look away, but he simply pursued his passion.

Do you know your passion; what moves you, what stirs you or gets you angry? However, this is not towards violence but a peaceful solution. Using Dr. King's words; *"meeting physical force with soul force"*. This was what gave Dr. King the Nobel Peace Prize in 1964, at a young age of 35, for civil rights activism against social injustice and racial inequality, all without any violence or subtle call for it. His strengths were in his oratory speeches, in his emotional intelligent speeches and in his godly sincerity.

HIS PHILOSOPHY

The philosophy of a person speaks of what dictates or governs how and what someone believes. It also speaks of how he relates, what motivates him, his concepts of life and his values and why he reasons the way he does. Likewise, having a philosophical attitude is one that could make you to have composure and calmness in the presence of trouble or annoyance. This is what Dr. King possessed and also imparted in others.

His philosophy describes how someone leading a movement could still write a peaceful and non-violent letter from the prison. This was after black people's homes and churches had been destroyed and he was still able to calm his followers. He had been severally insulted by ungodliness, insulted by injustice and racial inequality, but he remained calm and resolute in the face of opposition and injustice.

What could make a person to do such a thing or have such peace in the midst of turmoil? It was his belief and confidence to see all people live and co-exist side by side. Remember, he was a Minster of the gospel of Christ Jesus, and indeed, he lived up to that mandate given to him to the extent that today, his life and philosophy is still impacting people's lives all over the world.

Therefore, whatever your passion, make sure you hold unto a philosophy that is bigger and greater than you. It is in this way you would be able to leave a lasting legacy for humanity, even for those that hated you.

So, stay with your passion but have a philosophy that is beyond your strength so that you can have a legacy, even a legacy that will outlast you. What is your philosophy of life? This is part of what you will derive strength from, even as you strive to stand out in life, make an impact and a difference in life. This is part of what we can learn and emulate from the life of Dr. King. He kept speaking and standing against what he knew was injustice, ungodliness, inequality and prejudice. He rightly referred to God as a God of justice. Do you believe that too?

HIS DREAM

Dr. Martin Luther King was a man with a dream. How important is it for you to have a personal dream. A dream that is going to motivate you, keep you going and give you a sense of purpose. Dr. King had a dream and he walked and ran after his dream in order to see it fulfilled.

> *"I have a dream that my four little children will one day live in a nation where they will not be judged by the colour of their skin but by the content of their character"*
> *(Dr. Martin Luther King Jr.)*

"I Have a Dream" is a public speech delivered by Martin Luther King Jr on 28 August 1963, in which he calls for an end to racism in the United States. Delivered to over 250,000 civil rights supporters from the steps of the Lincoln Memorial during the 'March on Washington', the speech was a defining moment of the American Civil Rights Movement.

Dr. King was a dreamer and also watched over his dream as it were to see it come to pass. When you dream of what you want to see, whether in your life, home, community or nation, you need to keep watching those dreams until they come to fulfilment. Just as you are what you think, you are also what you dream. In other words, if what you think is your passion, what infuriates you that you think you must give solution to? That very thing that you think of passionately will soon engulf you and be part of you.

This is what could later become your dream and drives you on the journey of destiny. It is either going to carry you, sustain you, drive you or makes you to fly; this medium is what I called a dream.

Dr. King kept seeing what he had dreamt of. He saw that character will be the final judge and not the colour of your skin. He saw racial equality and social justice and not injustice, just because he believed justice will always prevail. You and I can keep hope alive, that we can defeat ungodliness and every injustice with conviction in our heart. You just have to be convinced that we have the divine capability to achieve the vision and the blessing of humanity.

> *"I have seen the promised land. I may not get there with you. But I want you to know that we, as a people, will get to the promised land"*
> *(Dr. Martin Luther King)*

Dr. King saw beyond the present, as a man full of dream and vision for a tomorrow that is bright for his people. The promised land he saw, like Moses, was the desired expectation for the freedom of black people from every ungodliness, injustice, racial inequality and prejudice.

Having fulfilled his part, he laid down the baton. Who is going to stand up for the good of the community and for the love of the nation?

MARY SLESSOR

Have you ever heard of Mary Slessor?

Mary Slessor was a Scottish lady who, despite the situation in her personal life, chose to live in another part of the world. This was because she was not indifferent to was happening in Africa. This simple lady from a poor slum in Dundee, Scotland left her country just to stop the killing of twins.

Mary Slessor was a Scottish missionary to Africa who championed the fight against destroying of lives. This was even before the United Nations Charter as she had simply lived beyond her time. This was because she was angry at what she was hearing and seeing. She was furious and angry at the injustice and ungodliness around her in Calabar, Nigeria.

It would have been easy for her to have said, I don't care for Africa, I would just survive here. After all, she was from the slums herself. Even though Mary was never married, yet she could feel the frustration of a mother whose children had been killed because they were born twins.

She moved to the Calabar region of Nigeria at the age of 28, converting her frustration into compassion. She lived in the same conditions as Africans and among the Efik people of Nigeria.

Mary Slessor sacrificed her personal comfort; she gave up on the dream of ever getting married. But in exchange for that she saved millions of twins. Have you ever seen twins from Africa before? That might be as a result of the efforts of Mary Slessor. Before her effort, it was the norm not to allow the two of them to survive, one always had to die.

Many people lived in the days of Mary Slessor, many more probably heard about the human sacrifice in Africa, yet only this poor Scottish lady converted her anger into constructive energy. Thanks to her, today's mothers can see their twin children grow up. It could be said that she brought civilization to that part of Africa through her sacrificial service to humanity.

For her efforts, she was eventually known as the White Queen of Okoyong. She died in Calabar in 1915 with no biological family or children of her own, but she became the mother of a whole nation. That is what happens when we convert insults and anger into constructive actions.

Dear readers, I would like to challenge you to look around your community, society and country. Is there anything that is irritating you? That might just be the very thing you are supposed to confront.

Have you noticed anything that frustrates you? Maybe God wants you to address it. What angers you in your community? That anger might be the subtle voice of God bringing your attention to the burden of His heart. If you would respond to the leading of God, you could end up becoming a Moses in your class, in your generation, your sphere of influence, in your promised land for millions of people worldwide.

"Throughout history, it has been the inaction of those who could have acted; the indifference of those who should have known better; the silence of the voice of justice when it mattered most; that has made it possible for evil to triumph" (Haile Selassie)

HER IMPACT

As Mary Slessor left Scotland for Calabar, Nigeria in 1886 as a missionary, her effort to stop the killing of twins was what really aroused her anger. An anger that was justified by the steps she took to stop such ungodliness, injustice and crime against humanity.

At that time, for every twin given birth, one of them was believed to be evil. However, since the evil child was not known among the two, then, they just abandoned both in the forest or out rightly killed them both. So, what she did was that she requested through the local authority to adopt those children. This was how Mary Slessor became the mother of hundreds or even thousands of children because she had adopted them.

'LET THE LIVING LIVE'

You likewise can follow in the pattern and lifestyle of Mary Slessor by making sure you let the living live. This implies what you could do to impact the living and would enable them to truly live.

Mary Slessor refused to have the living killed but made sure they remain alive up until today because of her tireless efforts. You too can do the same, go and make a difference. The world will be a better place and humanity will be better for it if you desire to do something. Do something about what infuriates you in the society, do something to impact the people and make a difference. Perhaps that could be the reason why you are still alive. Imagine, after the Bill of the abolition of the slave trade was finally passed in Parliament, a few days after that, William Wilberforce passed on.

So, don't pass on, until your 'Bill' has been passed;

your 'bill' for the sake of someone, a people, a city or a nation you are meant to impact. Get provoked to do something positive about the negative things you see around you. Get provoked at the ungodliness, injustice and all kinds of discrimination in the society, and humanity will be the better for this, just because you made a positive impact.

CHAPTER FOUR

THE
REFORMERS

THE REFORMERS

MARTIN LUTHER

Martin Luther, the German Reformer, sensed a great deal of frustration towards the teachings and practices of the Roman Catholic Church. He was definitely not the only one who was frustrated by those practices in his days. However, while others whinged and complained about their frustrations, Martin Luther decided to take the bull by the horn.

He built a system by which he was going to set humanity free from the deception of religion. Today, as a result of the life and ministry of Martin Luther, almost a billion people worldwide regarded themselves as Protestants. A whole denomination was named after him. Lutheranism today constitutes over 80 million adherents.

This is what happens when we decide to do something with our frustrations. Those people who only complain have nothing to show but those who act on their frustrations become Fathers of nations. These fathers simply give birth to solutions; something that moves the nation forward.

Are you insulted and irritated by the political situations in your country? God might be telling you to address them. Becoming a politician might not be the only way to address a political situation; it might just be enough for you to set up a mechanism of removing those things that irritate you from the government. At times, you simply need to speak out about what you see. At other times you might need to set up a structure or a system to address the issue. The bottom line is that you must turn your frustration into something constructive.

Too many people simply vent their emotions about the things that are wrong in their society. They whine, curse and complain, yet do nothing constructive to fix the situation. The point I am making is that your frustrations are not by accident. They are permitted to so overwhelm you that they could be used to better the lives of people around you and society in general.

It is no longer news that Martin Luther spearheaded the reformation that rocked and swept throughout the Roman Catholic world. Martin Luther had the audacity to challenge the supreme authority of the papacy, just as he was backed by Heaven's authority and power.

This he was able to do because Luther was infuriated and insulted by the ungodliness, the corruption, the injustice and wickedness of his time. Martin Luther was backed by Heaven's authority and grace; he was able to bring about a great change, not only to the Christian world, but to the world in general.

Martin Luther's reformation campaign began in 1517 and the change, the truth, the light and the development it brought are still with us today. Just because one man who stood for the truth, progress and development, felt angry by the ungodliness of his time.

He was able to challenge the status quo; therefore, he brought illumination, progress and development to the whole world. This further solidifies the fact that it is those that are insulted by the ungodliness, insulted by the injustice, insulted by the corruption and evil around them that make a change in their society and eventually their generation.

In this chapter, we shall further look into the life of Martin Luther and the lives of other individuals, who can also be referred to as reformers. They all lived in different generations but they were all irritated by different things; by ungodliness, injustice and other vices in their society, nations and generations and they made a positive change.

HIS BELIEVE AND MOTIVATION

Born in Eisleben, Germany in 1483, Martin Luther went on to become one of Western history's most significant figures. Luther spent his early years in relative anonymity as a monk and scholar. But in 1517, Luther penned a document attacking the Catholic Church's corrupt practice of selling "indulgences" to absolve sin. His "95 Theses" which propounded two central beliefs—that the Bible is the central religious authority and that humans may reach salvation only by their faith and not by their deeds—was to spark the Protestant Reformation.

Although these ideas had been advanced before, Martin Luther codified them at a moment in history ready for religious reformation. The Catholic Church was then divided and Protestantism soon emerged and shaped by Luther's ideas. His writings changed the course of religion and cultural history in the West.

Meanwhile, the Catholic Church's practice of granting "indulgences" to provide absolution to sinners became increasingly corrupt. Indulgence-selling had been banned in Germany, but the practice continued unabated. In 1517, a Friar named Johann Tetzel began to sell indulgences in Germany to raise funds to renovate St. Peter's Basilica in Rome.

Martin Luther's motivation to stand for the truth was born simply out of his strong desire to see the people set free from bondage of ignorance. This German monk's questioning of the Catholic dogma led to the Protestant Reformation. He felt furious at the doctrines that were perpetrated by the Roman Catholic Church - the selling of 'indulgencies'. Martin Luther was simply an angry man, who was irritated by the whole system of the church. He was even angry at the ungodly acts of the Catholic practice by not allowing the people to have Bibles.

Martin Luther had a genuine and holy anger against unrighteousness, ungodliness, every injustice and greed being practiced by the papacy. He could see that the heart and system did not reflect Christ nor glorified Him, though His name was mentioned on their lips.

He was supposed to study Law - the career he started but later jettisoned. The reason he actually left studying law was as a result of the way he survived a bolt of lightning that nearly struck him. He vowed to God that, if he was delivered, he will become a monk. So, when he was delivered from this deadly storm, he left his pursuit of becoming a lawyer and went into the Monastery.

Martin Luther as a monk was angry at the practice of selling indulgences by the papacy. He believed this practice was born out of greed and not the gospel of Christ. Martin Luther's anger against the unholy practice and towards the ungodliness of his time was the motivating force behind all that he did for the LORD. What is your anger towards? Is it a right or a righteous cause? Follow after the example of Martin Luther who purposed to go after the unpopular path and deliver humanity from the path of destruction and ungodliness. Everyone who thinks he has a message, or convinced that he needs to make a difference, then such an individual needs to keep standing and stay with such a vision like Martin Luther.

'THE 95 THESES'

Committed to the idea that salvation could be reached through faith and by divine grace, Luther vigorously objected to the corrupt practice of selling indulgences. Acting on this belief, he wrote the "Disputation on the Power and Efficacy of Indulgences," also known as "The 95 Theses," a list of questions and propositions for debate.

According to historical belief, on 31 October 1517, Luther defiantly nailed a copy of his 95 Theses to the door of the Wittenberg Castle church. The reality was probably not so dramatic; Luther more likely hung the document on the door of the church matter-of-factly to announce the ensuing academic discussion around it that he was organizing.

The 95 Theses, which would later become the foundation of the Protestant Reformation, were written in a remarkably humble and academic tone, questioning rather than accusing. The overall thrust of the document was nonetheless quite provocative. The first two of the theses contained Luther's central idea, that God intended believers to seek repentance and that faith alone, and not deeds, would lead to salvation. The other 93 theses, a number of them directly criticizing the practice of indulgences supported these first two.

Martin Luther's belief was the basis for his actions. Without being grounded in his belief, he would not have been able to take the steps that he took for the freedom of the Body of Christ. He knew that there was a need for reformation and he was readily available to be used of the LORD.

His 95 thesis were founded on his 2 central beliefs: that the Bible is the central religious authority for the Church of Christ and secondly, he stated that man can achieve salvation only by faith, through grace and not by their deeds. On these central beliefs is what the Protestant Reformation began and built on.

The Protestant Reformation, for your information, also brought with it other developments to humanity. Yes, with the arrival of Light comes development. The printing technology which began in Germany came with the dawn of the light of reformation. This was how it was possible to have the Bible printed and many were able to have access to the Bible through the work of Martin Luther. He spent 10 years translating the New Testament Bible to German.

How would you impact your generation with your godly belief? It is time for people to arise, people who will stand for what they believe and live for. We are in the time and generation that black is called white and white is called black. Stand for the truth, live for the truth and stand against every ungodliness and injustice.

HIS TRIAL, VICTORY AND IMPACT

Martin Luther was a man of pain. He faced great trial in the hand of papacy authority. However, he stood for what he believed in and with his conviction. If anyone is willing to be tried for what he believed, then, his belief is what is being listened to and facing trial.

Martin Luther's victory was the victory for the truth.

It was and still is the victory for the Bible - the Word of God to be followed solely and completely. In all his trials and the danger he passed through, he came out victorious. He won the battles of his life and he fulfilled his destiny. He accomplished his course.

MARTIN LUTHER'S IMPACT AND LEGACY

Luther was the central figure of the Protestant Reformation. There were religious reformers prior to him. However, it was Luther who brought the reformation to fruition and defined its essence. Today, Luther stands as a great influence to billions of Christians all over the world.

According to excerpts from the world encyclopedia, paralleling the ancient Israelite prophets Ezra, Nehemiah and Malachi who reconstructed Judaism after its Babylonian captivity, Luther sought to restore Christianity's foundation of faith following what he termed "the Babylonian Captivity of the Church." His efforts were partially successful. Christianity rid itself of certain corrupt practices, such as the selling of indulgences, but was ultimately divided into Protestant and Catholic camps. Luther was an unyielding proponent of Christian liberty and unleashed forces that accentuated ideological chaos, the triumph of nationalism and religious intolerance.

Luther's doctrine of justification by faith alone, sola fides, remains his most lasting theological contribution. It defined salvation as a new relationship with God, not based on any human work of merit but on absolute trust in the Divine promise of forgiveness for the sake of Christ. Here, Luther was a pioneer in reviving the Hebraic dimension of Christian faith that held that God's

Word trumped all else. To Luther, Christianity had become Hellenized, subject to philosophy and humanistic manipulation.

He believed that work-based righteousness had objectified faith making salvation an impersonal mechanized process. His own "evangelical breakthrough" was the result of a series of intense personal encounters with scripture. In this respect, Luther restored the subjective aspect of Christian experience. His critics maintained that this led to unbridled individualism.

BIBLE LEGACY

Luther translated the Bible into German to make it more accessible to the common people. He began the task of translating the New Testament in 1521, during his stay in the Wartburg Castle. It was completed and published in September 1522.

Luther's 1534 Bible translation was also profoundly influential on William Tyndale, who, after spending time with Luther in Wittenberg, published an English translation of the New Testament. In turn, Tyndale's translation was foundational for the King James Bible, thus, Luther's Bible influenced the most widely used English Bible translation, the King James Version.

POLITICAL LEGACY

Luther's political legacy is entwined with the formation of modern democracy. The teaching that an individual is ultimately accountable to God and responsible for his or her fate, created a basis for moral self-direction that set the tone for the entire reformation. Democracy requires self-directed and self-sufficient people. His emphasis on reading the Bible and other literary works also led to the development of people capable of understanding political literature and debating political issues.

KINGDOM LIGHT BEARER

Martin Luther's life was a phenomenon. He was a great pillar to the gospel of the Lord Jesus Christ. He was a reformer indeed; he brought Light to the darkness of his days. This was because he was furious at the corrupt and deluded established authority of the papacy. He chose to stand on the side of the Lord and was used mightily by Him. What are you standing for and what are you furious about that you want a change? The Lord is still looking for many Martin Luthers today that will stand for Him.

SAUL OF TARSUS

Saul was a zealous man according to the law. He was a devoted Pharisee and ready to do anything in order to protect the law and the traditions of the fathers. He can be said to be an angry man, yes, angry with anything or anyone that acted contrary to the law and traditions he held in high esteem. That was the life of Saul of Tarsus. He was angry at the gospel of the Lord Jesus, because he felt it was setting itself against the law and the traditions of the fathers.

Saul was fighting against something, though wrongly and ignorantly. However, he had the audacity to stand and even die, if need be, for the law and the traditions of Judaism, which he had upheld and promoted for the most part of his years. It was obvious Saul was on a wrong path; at least he was angry at something he believed in. In my opinion, this was an asset to the Kingdom of the Lord as this was later used for the right cause.

HIS BELIEF

"I am verily a man which am a Jew, born in Tarsus, a city in Cilicia, yet brought up in this city at the feet of Gamaliel, and taught according to the perfect manner of the law of the fathers, and was zealous toward God, as ye all are this day. And I persecuted this way unto the death, binding and delivering into prisons both men and women"

Acts 22: 3, 4

Saul was a man whose belief drove him to the point of trying to destroy the gospel of Christ. He was a passionate man; he stood firmly with what he believed; what he had convictions for. What is your conviction on spiritual truth today, even on social issues and are you willing to be labelled along with your conviction?

His belief made him to do so many things. His belief made him to be zealous for God. His belief made him to be persecuting the Church of Christ. His belief made him to imprison so many believers in Christ. His belief also made him to give orders for the death of believers. Saul was angry at anything; a person, an organization, an institution or a belief that set itself against the belief of Judaism.

He felt insulted by the beliefs around him that did not follow the pattern of the fathers' traditions. He did this within Jerusalem and outside Jerusalem and Judea. This shows how a belief system or a conviction could rule and take control of a person, whether it is a right or wrong belief.

What is your belief or conviction about the occurrences around you in the society and in the nation? Is it what you have a passion for? Is it what propels you to stand for the truth and godliness? Is it what can make people to be spiritually or socially free or something that will impact their lives for good?

HIS ENCOUNTER

"And Saul, yet breathing out threatening and slaughter against the disciples of the Lord, went unto the high priest. And desired of him letters to Damascus to the synagogues, that if he found any of this way, whether they were men or women, he might bring them bound unto Jerusalem. ...It is hard for thee to kick against the pricks. Arise and go into the city, and it shall be told thee what thou must do"

Acts 9: 1,2, 5b,6b

Saul of Tarsus was fighting for the protection and advancement of the law and the tradition of the fathers. In his own eyes he was fighting for a just cause but was actually fighting against His Creator and Lord.

Saul as a man can be characterized in this way; he had energy, he was focused, he was determined; he even endangered himself while fighting for what was wrong, which he thought ignorantly was right. All these characteristics found in Saul will now be re-channeled towards the righteous cause of the Lord.

What have you got in you? I could boldly tell you that they are basically there not just for you. Charisma and strength are in you because of your assignment; the people you are sent to; the people you are to fight for and the society you are to impact. Maybe you can speak so you can be a voice for the voiceless. Probably, you could shed tears easily and it might be evident that you will be able to show compassion to so many people.

JUSTICE OF MAN AND JUSTICE OF GOD

Saul was fighting for what I called justice according to the 'gospel' of man. However, man's idea, man's philosophy, man's understanding and man's endeavour outside of God is futile and it is worship of man. However, man needs to receive God's idea of doing things since man was created to worship the LORD alone.

This was the scenario and situation Saul found himself in and which he entangled himself in. He involved himself in a religion that God should be the centre of, but he eventually pushed out the Lord God from that same religion. This was a religion in which God was supposed to be the centre of worship in the first place.

"He loves righteousness and justice: The earth is full of the loving kindness of the Lord"

Psalm 33: 5 (ASV)

God loves justice and He desires mankind to love the same. Saul was seeking his own justice, by his own hands and effort, leaving aside the justice of God. Saul put himself in the position of God instead of placing God at the centre of worship. Instead of Saul continuing in his campaign for justice, God introduced him to the true gospel just as Dr. Martin Luther King said that "God is a God of justice".

The gospel revealed the love of God and how He

placed all the sin of mankind on the Lord Jesus. This is justice indeed because of the righteous requirement that has been met in Christ Jesus. God is a God of justice. So, Saul or any other individual for that matter is not needed to fight for God. The price has already being paid which is the blood of Christ Jesus.

HIS ORDEAL AND IMPACT

Saul who was later known as Paul went through a great ordeal for the sake of the true gospel. Paul spent the remaining part of his life to fight for the true justice and to spread it. From that moment on after that encounter, Paul began to live and to be motivated for something else. He went through trials and difficulties for the true gospel; living and fighting for it.

Do you know that for everyone who is fighting for evil and destructive cause and championing injustice, there are potentially one million people that can stand, speak and fight against their evil and ungodly ideology. In other words, there are more people like you who could stand against ungodliness and injustice in this generation, than those sponsoring them. This is the campaign; this is what you and I must be champions for.

HAPPINESS AND THE RIGHT CAUSE

"Then Paul stretched forth the hand, and answered for himself: I think myself happy, King Agrippa, because I shall answer for myself this day before you… Whereupon, O king Agrippa, I was not disobedient unto the heavenly vision"

Acts 26: 1b, 2, 19

This was Saul now Paul rehearsing his encounter with the Lord and what he has gone through. He categorically stated that he was not disobedient to the heavenly vision. Even if he chose to, I do not think he would be able to do so because the vision had already become part of him.

For this reason, Paul was able to say publicly that he was filled with happiness as a result of the way his has been. He saw happiness in what he was championing; a movement that no power could overcome. He derived happiness from what he saw his life had become. This is true happiness. Your heart is satisfied with what you have chosen to do, which is impacting the people, those you have seen and those you have not seen. This is true happiness. Even in chain and in prison, Paul was full of happiness.

Are you happy? Do you want to be happy like Paul? Then, take a stand on what is just, what is right and on what is godly. There is happiness; there is satisfaction in fighting for the right and just cause. Speak out for someone, stand up for someone, impact a life and determine to be a ladder for someone or a people.

PAUL'S IMPACT

The life of Paul and the work he carried out was that of a Reformer and one with distinction. Christendom is better for it as the world was turned 'right side up' and not upside down, as his antagonists said about him.

He suffered lack, in penury, in shipwreck, in danger day and night, and he was still able to stand and he gave all of his life to what he believed. What are you willing to be sold out to? What is the coming generation going to remember you for? Tomorrow surely start today.

This suggests that there is no one that cannot make an impact in this world. One of the criteria is to be irritated by something that needs positive change. That is, be angry at vices in the society, be furious at injustice, have a godly philosophy, hold unto it dearly and stand unwavering for that cause. This is the way to impact a generation.

NELSON MANDELA AND THE APARTHEID SYSTEM

Nelson Mandela has become a household name all around the world. How did he become such a global hero? It was insult!

Living in apartheid South Africa, Mandela could not but feel insulted and irritated by what was going on around him. Instead of just voicing out his frustration and anger, he built a system of response through which he was frustrated by could be addressed.

He dreamt of seeing a democratic South Africa. For this great wish of his to come to a reality, he had to serve 27 years in prison. Thereafter, this enabled him to become the first black President of an independent South Africa. He was able to go through the struggle, the loneliness and the pain and eventually come out victorious.

Yes, frustrations do come. Irritations will surely attack you and insults would be hurled at you. It is your response that makes the difference. A constructive response will bring about change now and for eternity. However, just an emotional response of sentiments will only lead to tiredness and weariness. Nelson Mandela's life is worthy of emulation.

Some people live in the society and pay little or no

attention to the social ills of their nation. They are not irritated by them, they are not angered by them and they are not even frustrated by them. They simply go about their daily activities oblivious of the social realities of their surroundings.

Meanwhile, some other people might be concerned about the social malfunctions of their city. They talk about it all the time; they express their anger and frustrations. The important thing however is that these sentiments are gathered together and turned into a voice of reformation. Please don't waste your anger anymore but convert it to a positive action!

The apartheid system in South Africa perpetuated so much injustice, racial prejudice, oppression and segregation where non-whites were not allowed to participate in the national vote.

People were segregated in their own land because a minority had the military power to oppress the people instead of protecting them. Nelson Mandela rose to leadership position among his colleagues and lived an exemplary life before them. With his activism against apartheid, he was sentenced to life imprisonment in 1963 and was there for 27 years.

The life of Nelson Mandela could be said to be the life of an angry man, towards injustice, oppression and barbaric manners of treating black people or non-whites in South Africa. He decided to take his destiny and the destiny of his people in his own hands. That is, he simply took responsibility for the freedom and wellbeing of his people. He simply lived for his people.

This is evident that those who fight for social justice and the rights of people will count any other thing as unimportant. This is the way Mandela lived his life. He held his destiny and that of his people in his hands, and when he came out of prison in 1990, he gave that destiny and life back into the hands of the people.

> "I stand here before you not as a prophet but as a humble servant of you, the people. Your tireless and heroic sacrifices have made it possible for me to be here today. I therefore place the remaining years of my life in your hands"
> (Nelson Mandela)

He now sees the people as the custodian of his destiny and that of theirs. That was the impulse of the statement made by this humble man. He placed the rest of his life in the hands of his people. This is a statement that would make people believe in you if they know you mean what you say.

LESSONS FOR HUMANITY

We will always learn vital lessons from one another as the life, the passion, the struggle and the victory for Nelson Mandela is an important one. Yes, vital lessons because those who have gone ahead and who are possessed with characteristics that are worth emulating will always and will continue to be sought for and remain as treasures and treated like a memorial precious stones.

Likewise, Mandela was able to use forgiveness to overcome evil. He was able to use peace to suppress war and calamity. Such an individual with such qualities is someone to be emulated in that respect. Likewise, you can be a person with a strong passion or holy anger and be furious in a way that will make the society safer, godly, with social justice and equity.

Here are some quotes of Mandela which speaks of his philosophy, his belief, his stand on some issues in society, his thought pattern and his life experience.

"If you want to make peace with your enemy, you have to work with your enemy. Then he becomes your partner".

"There is no passion to be found playing small - in settling for a life that is less than the one you are capable of living".

"It always seems impossible until it's done".

"Courageous people do not fear forgiving, for the sake of peace".

"There is no easy walk to freedom anywhere, and many of us will have to pass through the valley of the shadow of death again and again before we reach the mountaintop of our desires".

"To deny people their human rights is to challenge their very humanity".

THE REFORMERS

All these men have become institutions among mankind. Yes, their lives have become institutions for others to surely learn from; the reformers - Martin Luther, Paul (formerly Saul of Tarsus) and Nelson Mandela. An individual who had set a pathway for millions, even billions, such is the life of Martin Luther. Someone who had brought light and enlightenment to mankind through the light of the Gospel; such is the life of Paul. Someone who went through pain to bring great gain to his people and nation; such is the life of Nelson Mandela.

Where are you standing and what act are you playing

or ready to play in the scene of life? We are all suppose to act on this stage on this side of eternity and one day your own scripts will be completed and you would be expected to have carried out all the acts in your scripts.

Therefore, stand out, stand up, speak out and impact a life, a people, a society or a generation. You might just be acting out your own scripts which you were meant to carry out. This is your time, this is your stage and it is time to carry out the role that could impact humanity for many generations to come.

CHAPTER FIVE

PURPOSEFUL LIFE

PURPOSEFUL LIFE

"If you don't stand for something, you will fall for everything" (Ralph Waldo Emerson)

"The purpose of life is not to be happy. It is to be useful, to be honorable, to be compassionate, and to have it make some difference that you have lived and lived well" (Ralph Waldo Emerson)

From the above quotes, it unveils that life is more than being happy; it is to impact lives and live for the good of your generation. However, it is only for those who feel insulted by ungodliness, injustice, corruption and darkness can make a positive change and impact their generation.

To be able to impact the society and to be an agent of change, you have to make yourself available to serve. To be honorable, you have to make sacrifices for others. To be compassionate, you have to forget your own comfort zone and live well because you live beyond yourself. These can only be carried out by those who have given all to make a change. This is how to live a purposeful and impactful life.

What bothers you today or gives you concerns could be a signpost to your purpose in life. In this chapter, we shall look into what you need to be able to fulfil your purpose in life.

We will also look into examples of individuals who fulfilled their life's purpose because they felt insulted by the corruption, the ungodliness, by the injustice and evil around them.

"The purpose of life is not to be happy – but no matter, but to be productive, to be useful, and to have it make some difference that you have lived at all" (Leo Rosten)

In most countries, people only care about the economy as it affects their pockets. Moreover, not too many individuals carry the burden to actually step out and address the economic challenges of their nation. If you see your country going through economic problems, the best thing to do is to come up with a strategy, plan and vision of how to affect the economy of the nation, rather than simply fixing your own individual economic problem.

With this kind of attitude, it is easy to bring a lasting solution to the economic woes of a nation because the individuals, who are not happy with the economy, respond by contributing to it. That constructive attitude would definitely enhance the economic development of that nation. If you are frustrated with the elite of your society, do something about it, start an educational program, organize seminars, symposiums and colloquiums. You could let them see what they have not seen before; show them how and when they could be relevant to the growth and development of their nation.

If you think the political parties are a disappointment, it's not a big deal - simply do something about it. Don't just vent your emotions and feelings without proffering a solution. Come up with a program for the political parties; bring insight, understanding and wisdom to them. Share the opinions in regards to their actions. Everything can be fixed simply by converting your frustrations into constructive contributions.

If you notice drunkards and you feel frustrated about them, it could be a pointer that God wants you to fix them. Some people might not even notice them even though they encounter them daily on the streets, still they don't see them.

Whereas, you not only see them but you are concerned and troubled by their state. That means, God is trying to get your attention and show you that you are needed here. Don't wait for somebody to come and fix it, you should endeavour to fix it. Maybe you could do the following: start a rehabilitation centre for the drug and alcohol addicts. Teach them until they become leaders and then send them back for a victorious harvest in the society. When everybody contributes a change to what he or she notices, it is then we will change our world.

- Are you insulted by the ungodliness of your nation?
- Are you furious by the injustice in the society?
- Are you insulted by the inequalities of your land?
- Are you concerned by the assault of evil in your country?
- Do you ever notice that lives are being destroyed by drugs and drug dealers?

- Does corruption bother you?
- Where is your holy anger regarding the negative environment around you?
- What is your frustration provoking you to, fear or faith?
- Are you a modern David for your nation, who would be so insulted by the challenge of Goliath, and become a deliverer for your country?
- Is your destiny hidden in your frustrations?
- Do you possess a holy anger like Moses?
- Would you prove to be a man of faith like Gideon?
- Do you have the stones that would slay the Goliaths of your land?

We will now look at different individuals who have demonstrated and depicted a life of purpose. What characterised their lives? They lived for others. Therefore, I submit to you that to live a life of purpose you will have to live for others.

DAVID: A MAN WITH A DIFFERENT HEART

David was foremost king of Israel. His life today is an institution and is still currently being studied and followed up whether in Israel among the Jews or all over the world.

What is so unique or special about this man, the son of Jesse? He became the most celebrated king and role model for other kings in the whole of Israel.

DAVID SERVED

"For David after he had served his own generation by the will of God, fell on sleep, and was laid unto his fathers..."

Acts 13:36

Yes, David the king served. That implies that he saw the throne as an opportunity to serve. Do you know what it means to serve? Today, everybody wants to be master without ever serving anyone. Nelson Mandela was in prison for a major part of his life because he wanted to serve his people.

David served Israel as king. He fought wars, kept the people secured and brought security and prosperity during his time. The Scripture says he served his generation after the will of God who chose him. How many kings after him made great impact on their people like he did? David was a servant and he served the Lord and was king over the people.

There are great things leaders can learn from David which could help them to serve their people. David always remembered where God brought him from – from caring for the sheep. He was not perfect but he was a man after God's heart. How great would it be for leaders to emulate the life David lived, a life of a servant-king?

There is satisfaction in serving. The best you could offer is to serve others; serve someone, serve your church, serve your community, serve the society and serve the nation. The more service we give to others, the more the satisfaction we derive. Serve and be a voice to the voiceless, serve and defend the defenseless, serve to promote social justice, serve to stand against ungodliness, serve,

serve and serve.

DAVID THE SELFLESS

David was concerned and so he acted to protect the interest of Israel after his death. He demonstrated something that was the first of its kind in Israel and which was never repeated by any other king after him. Today, some royal families did it to their happiness and security of their kingdom.

"So when David was old and full of days, he made Solomon his son king over Israel"

1 Chronicles 23: 1

What he did was that he made his son Solomon king in his very presence. This was a very selfless attitude and acts for him to abdicate his throne to his son. David was a pacesetter for all in his class and for those who do not even believe in him. David abdicated the throne to his son Solomon and this was security not only for Solomon, but for peace and tranquility in Israel, even after he was no longer alive.

David was mindful of posterity and he acted in a way that could take care of that. Anyone therefore that will make a difference would have to put others ahead of them; put others first. This is the way to live and make great impact needed in any society.

DAVID'S LIFE FULL PURPOSE

"Thus David the son of Jesse reigned over all Israel. And he died in a good old age, full of days, riches and honour"

1 Chronicle 29: 26, 28

David was a fulfilled man; he lived his life fulfilling his purpose. What characterized this? It was basically his service to the people being rooted in the fear of the Lord. He was a worshiper of the Lord God.

His people sincerely loved him because they saw a sincerity that was genuine in him. Every leader therefore who has the interest of the people at heart must have something to learn from David. Learn from him on how to serve, how to win the heart of the people and how to take your nation to higher level than anyone else.

There was an occurrence in Israel few years ago as related by an international Pastor. At that time, the Jews in Israel were celebrating the achievements of David; a victorious king over Jerusalem. Then, according to the story, there was a man that made a public statement: "Why are these people celebrating David like this, was he not the same David that killed Uriah and took his wife". Information had it that, this man was a member of 'Knesset', a position that could be classified as a legislator in Israel, and because of his derogatory statement about someone highly honoured by the people, the very next day, his constituency recalled him.

David was not a perfect man, just as any man, but he has set before us an exemplary life. He was called a man after God's own heart.

Back to the story above, it reflected the way a typical Jew sees the life of David even up to today. If we will live a life that is plain before the people, whether you are a father, legislator, Pastor, king, governor or whoever, you will gain the respect and honour of your people.

Frequently, so many people are being insulted, segregated, dehumanized and deprived and constantly receiving injustice as payback. But you can stand out for them. This was part of what David did when individuals who have lost hope, came to him and they sought for comfort from him. Will you also stand or speak up for them? This was the kind of person David was, he was a man with a heart for the people. If you want to live a life of full purpose, then live for others, live for the people and live for generations to come.

DANIEL THE LEADER

Daniel was a young man taken as captive from Judah to Babylon. He eventually came to prominence under a divine orchestration and a divine purpose. Have you ever watched a fiction movie where someone was taken as a war captive to a foreign land and he eventually became a governor in that land? Well, this was not an invented story, this was the actual story of 'Daniel the wise'.

Daniel's purpose in life began or came to light when the king of the land was angry and furious. This scenario placed the life of Daniel in possible death. This was because there wasn't anyone who could solve the king's problem, to tell him his dream and to interpret it as well.

So the anger of the king was to bring a rare opportunity to Daniel. Daniel was simply insulted and challenged at the same time by the anger of king Nebuchadnezzar. The anger of the king was the stepping stone for Daniel to enter his full purpose.

"For this cause the king was angry and very furious, and commanded to destroy all the wise men of Babylon"

Daniel 2:12

This scenario was what motivated Daniel to go to his Lord for solution. I could well imagine that Daniel too was angry. Angry that he found himself in a foreign land, angry that the king wanted interpretation to a dream he never told anyone, and angry that he, a Jew, was serving an idolatrous king in a strange land.

Therefore, the anger of Nebuchadnezzar the king further exposed the anger in Daniel. The anger of the king was not reasonable and it could be described as over expectation or a desire of an over-ambitious king. He wanted his dream to be known by a mortal man and also interpreted for him.

However, the anger in Daniel was a justified one and in a way a necessary one. It was a necessary anger, because it pushed him to his Lord and to the Everlasting King, from whom all solutions come. So, don't waste your anger; don't underestimate the result of a right and positive anger. That could be the beginning of the result, the rest and the respect you needed.

"Then was the secret revealed to Daniel in a night vision. Then Daniel blessed the God of heaven"
Daniel 2: 19

The solution came as a result of the anger of someone called Daniel. It came against the ungodliness, injustice and unfair disposition of a mere mortal king. What is your anger directed to in this society or nation? You can turn it around and receive solution from the Lord, in order to impart the lives of men; to stop the death of many, to bring many from darkness and to bring freedom to many in bondage.

DANIEL THE SERVANT – LEADER

"Then Daniel requested of the king, and he set Shadrach, Meshach and Abednego, over the affairs of the province of Babylon: but Daniel sat at the gate of the king"

Daniel 2: 49

Another version says, *"... but Daniel served in the court of the king". Daniel 2: 49 (NET)*

What could be bigger than serving? What could be more honourable than seeking honour and position for others and not for you? Then, we may not necessarily look for too long, to search and find what made Daniel great and to last longer than others.

Daniel served three successive kings in the whole of the Babylonian empire; Nebuchadnezzar, Belshazzar and Darius. With all the privileges, honour and prestige accrued to Daniel, he never allowed that to get to his head. When every opportunity given to you is used to serve the people, you are on the path of life's purpose to the fullness.

JOB THE BUSINESSMAN

Job was a man who lived thousands of years ago and had a testimony that he served the Lord and did not fail to do what was right. He might not have been without any fault; however, his heart was right before the Lord. He had a heart that sought after God and also feared the Lord. Notwithstanding what he went through in life as an individual, he did not neglect those he needed to serve with his heart, his voice and with his hands.

In other words, serving others is one of the bases

for you to have or to enjoy a fullness of purpose in life. Moreover, to serve others is not only by hands but by mouth as well.

> *"I also could speak as ye do: if your soul were in my soul's stead, I could heap up words against you, and shake mine head at you. But I would strengthen you with my mouth, and the moving of my lips should assuage your grief"*
>
> *Job 16:4, 5*

The friends of Job spoke evil of Job and derided him. However, Job who should have been angry instead decided to do otherwise. He told them the exact thing he would do. He would strengthen them; he would energize them; he would build them up and not pull them down. I submit to you that there will come a time where you will be in a situation where you will be insulted by ungodly people and be where you will be face to face with the injustice of men.

This was the experience of Job, but he knew something the friends did not know, that he was only fulfilling his purpose in life. He knew God that knows all things and that God will be his focus and desire.

From the statement of Job, we could see that words can strengthen or pull down. Your words can therefore build a nation. Your voice can be made loud to speak against ungodliness and injustice and not promote it.

As it happened, Job decided to strengthen his friends by praying for them and his end was more glorious than before. Therefore, Job fulfilled his life's purpose; he stood his ground, he prayed for his accusers and he was vindicated at last. He was referred to as the greatest man in the whole of the East.

"Not for any injustice in mine hands:..."

Job 16: 17

Job was saying; no evil speaking of his friends in his mouth though he was continually insulted by them. Likewise, he said no injustice in his hands. He had not used his hands to steal from the people he was to serve; he had not used his hands to pull down the people's heads which he was supposed to lift up.

If you have experienced injustice and insulted by the ungodliness, then you are a candidate to stand against the same. Job was a man who fulfilled his life's purpose with his mouth and hands.

The opportunity given to you to make use of both your mouth and hands to build the home and society is enormous. These are the basic things needed to build either the home or the community. You need a good mouth and working hands. If you are ready to make a difference and shine, then you must be ready to pay the price by labouring rightly with your mouth and with hands.

ESTHER THE QUEEN

The time and the season that Esther came to the land where the Jews were held in captive was a timely one. When she came she thought she was just part of the number of the captives but she never knew she had a different purpose to fulfil. Esther was definitely oblivious of her divine assignment and destiny that was placed on her shoulder.

Esther's privilege and opportunity manifested because someone was angry and felt insulted. Opportunity is present when the heart of an individual is insulted or angry.

> *"But the queen Vashti refused to come at the king's commandment by his chamberlain: therefore the king was wroth, and his anger burned in him"*
>
> *Esther 1: 12*

The King of the Persian Empire was angry and insulted by the attitude and behaviour of his queen, Vashti. Therefore, she was dethroned and a new queen was sought. Therefore, information was sent to the all the provinces of the Persian Empire to invite potential ladies who could become queen and replace Vashti.

Whoever suggested to Esther to participate in becoming queen in a land she had been a slave or a captive all these years, did good to her. She was simply pushed into her life's purpose. By the way, every individual's purpose in life will always have others to support it. It could include the one that got angry, the one that was insulted and the one that announced or suggested to you to come into your destiny of making a difference.

Esther's life and all that she went through in the land of captivity were all part of what made her. You might have been insulted by injustice or even abused; all can still be turned into a new story and used as a pedestal that could bring you and make you an advocate for social justice, a champion for change and a voice for the less privileged.

To cut the long story short, Esther became the queen of the Persian Empire. She had set a standard for us all, that no matter your level in life you can still impact your people, even your world.

ESTHER AND THE JEWS' DESTINY

"... I also and my maidens will fast likewise, and so will I go in unto the king, which is not according to the law, and if I perish, I perish"

Esther 4:16

This statement reflected a girl who had put her life on the line. Why? It was because she chose to listen to someone who had displayed his anger towards the danger that was to come on the Jews. The person she listened to was her uncle, by name Mordecai. It was an anger born out of frustration. It was an anger that looked to God for change and deliverance.

This was what Esther shared with her uncle - anger. An anger to see to it that enough is enough and the Jews must no longer be victimised. So she decided to seek for a change in order to save the lives of millions of Jews and counted her life not as important if she could only make an attempt to save her people.

It was a display of this anger and confidence in the absolute power of God that delivered them from evil and the ungodliness of the land. This was what motivated her to seek God and she went ahead in the face of danger just to save her people. This was a decision born out of anger that set the nation of the Jews free from their enemies.

It was an anger that made her and others seek God in prayer and fasting and to seek deliverance from genocide. This is where the strength lies; anger to seek a change and confidence that you are a vessel in God's hand to bring change to the people.

CHAPTER SIX

INSULTED BY OPPRESSION

INSULTED BY OPPRESSION

The great and the mighty that use their assets and power to subjugate people are demonstrating oppression. Oppression is actually defined as the exercise of authority or power in a cruel or unjust manner.

I will like to state this analogy: Covetousness gives birth to violence, while violence gives birth to oppression. Covetousness is what I refer to as the grandfather of oppression. Moreover, when you see injustice among the nations, you will find out that the root cause is covetousness. Likewise, the architect and the father of war are covetousness of the leaders and of different interest groups fuelling war.

"And I said, hear, I pray you, ye heads of Jacob, and rulers of the house of Israel: is it not for you to know justice"

Micah 3:1

There are three words to take note in the above Scripture, they are, 'rulers', 'know' and 'justice'. In other words, if there is anything the leaders in the society or the nations must take note of is to know the importance of justice.

When justice is prioritized by any leader at any level then to give justice to the citizenry will always be at the back of the mind of such a leader. This is because the absence of justice anywhere is the presence of injustice everywhere. A leader must be taught or made to know the importance of justice for the people. The people must not be attacked by ungodliness and injustice in the society.

If there is any society where the leaders lack the knowledge and the importance of justice, then oppression will be a common neighbour of the citizens. Violence and oppression will come from the same source - injustice and covetousness. Covetousness breeds violence while injustice breeds oppression. In any society where injustice and covetousness is the order of the day, oppression and violence will thrive.

In other words, covetousness and injustice will produce the same results or fruits. Wherever you see covetousness, you will see injustice. The products of the two 'brothers', covetousness and injustice, are violence and oppression and they create more trouble and evil in society. This is the reason why every leader must have knowledge of justice so that violence and oppression will be stifled from the society.

If there is anyone or group of people who are expected to see that the people are no longer suppressed and insulted by oppression, they are the leaders. The leaders have the responsibility to protect and hold in high esteem the law and virtues of the land. However, before you run away with; "yes, tell them", I need to let you know that everyone is a leader in one way or the other. Whether as a leader in the home or among your team at work, or as a leader in your church group or on your street, you are a leader too. In other words, everyone is a leader on one level or another and is expected to be an influence. Therefore, when all these leaders in different capacity are produced and raised in the society, then the society will be the better for it. This is when violence and injustice will not produce oppression in the society.

LEVELS OF OPPRESSION

"They covet fields, and seize them; and houses, and take them away: and they oppress a man and his house, even a man and his heritage"

Micah 2:2

Oppression has been in existence as long as man himself has been in existence. A man oppresses another man, a man covets another man's possessions, and a man is violent to another man at whatever level, even if it means killing a fellow man.

SINGLE LEVEL OPPRESSION

When a man that is being oppressed I call it single level oppression. Ahab the king coveted a man's garden and his wife Jezebel helped him to actualize it by killing the owner himself of the field. As stated above, it is covetousness that makes a fellow man to do violence to another man. Likewise, injustice breeds oppression of all kinds.

FAMILY LEVEL OPPRESSION

When oppression gets to family level, the offspring of such a family is not safe. That is, they are open to oppression. It is pathetic today that a man and his house, which is his family, are being perpetrated. The oppressor is not only violent but even to his family. In one instance, a young boy was shot and killed instead of his father. This is an example of how family members can partake in violence and oppression in the society.

It is time someone stand up and speak out to decry violence and especially violence towards children. In other cases, the oppression towards the family is in the repossessing of the resources and properties of the house when the head of the family dies. Therefore, the widow and the fatherless children are left with nothing to live with. This is wickedness and oppression demonstrated. This practice is present in parts of Africa today. It is time for someone to arise and speak against this injustice, oppression and violence against women. It is time someone or a group stood up for social justice in this area. It could be you.

GENERATIONAL OPPRESSION

Looking at the word heritage in the above Scripture, it implies possessions that belong to someone by reason of birth. This is what someone has inherited. Therefore, heritage is meant to be for generations and to be transferred from one generation to the next.

Generational oppression begins when what is meant to be transferred to one offspring has been taken over by reason of oppression. In Africa today, land, plantation and other produce meant to be transferred to one generation has been destroyed by crude oil and through the negligence of international oil firms. Little or nothing is paid to the people because the people have no voice and are continually oppressed.

When a man or family is oppressed, it has become a generational oppression. It is now an oppression that goes beyond the lifetime of the man or family which now involves many families. This goes beyond the present and now into the future.

A young girl in Afghanistan fought for the future generation by standing up and speaking against the oppression for girls not to be educated.

Likewise, each one needs to do something, whether it is by impacting a generation or through your effort of advocacy. It is also good to know that every effort to impact someone or a generation will go a long way beyond human imaginations.

Let this generation arise; let the generation of those that have been oppressed arise so that others coming behind will not be oppressed. Many a times, steps you take or efforts you will make will keep speaking figuratively. It will make impact on generations to come. Let this generation, which has been insulted by ungodliness, oppression, violence and injustice, arise and learn from those that have gone ahead to lay a legacy for those coming behind.

MORDECAI AS A CASE STUDY

Mordecai was a man who felt insulted by oppression, ungodliness and injustice against his people, the Jews, in the land of captivity. He was so insulted by ungodliness, injustice and corruption that he refused to bow to a man known as Haman, who wanted all Jews killed.

No, Mordecai was not a proud man, he was only infuriated and displeased. For so long, he had been insulted by the ungodliness and the injustice he and his people faced while in captivity in the land of Persia.

"Surely oppression maketh a wise man mad ..."

Ecclesiastes 7:7

This was the experience of Mordecai.

Mordecai will be looked at further in this chapter how his life, principles, belief, faith and philosophy of life brought about the emancipation of the Jews, while in the land of bondage.

This shows and confirms that one man can surely change society, a nation and the world in general. This individual has been irritated by ungodliness, injustice, corruption and oppression around him that he was ready to make a difference.

"And when Haman saw that Mordecai bowed not, nor did him reverence, then was Haman full of wrath. And he thought to scorn to lay hands on Mordecai alone; for they had shewed him the people of Mordecai: wherefore Haman sought to destroy all the Jews that were throughout the whole kingdom of Ahasuerus, even the people of Mordecai"

Esther 3: 5, 6

Haman then went ahead to persuade the king to eliminate the Jews from his kingdom. What was the offence of these people? This was because of Mordecai. He was the one that reflected the Jewish law and custom and because he chose to keep his law in a foreign land. Haman wanted to make sure he took the life of every Jew by annihilating them. He planned to destroy the future generation of the Jews.

When someone gains the power and influence that Haman had at that time, it will not be difficult for him to do likewise. It will take a man of grace and wisdom like Mordecai to bring such a wicked person under control.

And the letters were sent by posts into all the king's provinces, to destroy, to kill, and to cause to perish, all Jews, both young and old, little children and women, in one day..."

Esther 3: 13

These are many generations that Haman had planned to destroy and to kill just because of ego. This is oppression in display; this is crime against humanity; this is genocide and racial cleansing already planned. He felt this group of people would become too powerful for him if he was in command in that kingdom. This was the reason Haman decided that they should be wiped off from the earth.

We still have that type of Haman today. On a lighter note, the name of Haman looks and sounds so much like 'human'. In other words, Haman is human. Human beings are full of ego, jealousy and destruction and will always want to elevate themselves above others. However, this is a wrong expression and a true human being will honour others created in the image of God, and will not oppress an image of the Lord.

We live in a society that if someone likes you and refuses to stand up and demand true human right and social justice, you might find yourself isolated and in the Dark Age.

A lot has been committed into your hands in order to be able to leave a good legacy for the coming generation. We are the generation that much has been given and impacted by those that have gone ahead in order for us to be able to give back as well.

Haman's decree which he got by manipulation had caused the life of every Jew to be in danger of genocide.

Mordecai was not just a Jew in that kingdom but was placed strategically to make a change for his people. In other words, every opportunity, every influence and affluence you possess, could not have been for you alone, but to act as a platform to impact a generation.

Don't be silent, don't feel unconcerned when you see people in society being overwhelmed by oppression. This was what Mordecai refused to do. Mordecai refused to be quiet and in addition to his prayer to the God of heaven and earth, he began to press the button he had in the 'high places'. However, the button he was pressing was not for him.

What Mordecai was after was for his people not to be wiped out, but to be preserved. When will we have someone who will have a revolution of order in our market and without having anything to do with the government?

When would someone stand up for the rights of those who suffer in the hands of petroleum firms that pollute farms and river without having anything to do with the government?

The ball is now in our hands, to either throw out or serve it and pass it on. This was what Mordecai did. He challenged Esther to act and not wait for the time the king would call her, but to take the destiny of her people in her hand. This was what Nelson Mandela did by choosing to go to the prison for 27 years.

Mordecai not only challenged his niece to act right with faith in the Lord, but he also went ahead to call all Jews into a solemn assembly of fasting and prayer. Before you know it, while combining supernatural force with natural force, help came for the Jews. The Jews, who was at the mercy of their killers, were now having the upper hand over their enemies.

Haman, who had prepared a device to hang Mordecai, was eventually himself hanged on it, including all members of his household.

This is the time to act, this is the time to speak, this is the time to deliberate, this is the time to set an example for others, and this is the time to receive help from above, to face the giants in the society who are swallowing people. This is a testament to the fact that light will always overcome darkness; it is a matter of time.

There are people around us who are 'swallowing' others with hunger, with oppression of different types, with injustice and discrimination. We need stand up to our responsibility and stand at the top of the corner without being harassed by the tyrants by choosing to make a difference. It's time to make a difference for a boy who was abandoned, for a girl who had lost it all and for a man or woman who had become helpless.

Stand up on your street and render community help. Stand up on your campus, not with a knife, cutlass or with a gun, but with a voice that will ring like a bell in the heart of the people. Welcome to a life indeed that will make impact upon somebody, a family, society, a race and the nation.

NEHEMIAH AS A CASE STUDY

Who was Nehemiah? Where was he coming from and what responsibility did he take upon himself for the sake of his people. What irritated him and how did he handle the insult?

Mordecai was in the land of captivity when he was

used to spearhead the safety and deliverance for the Jews. Nehemiah as well was in the land of captivity, serving in the palace when his heart was grieved, sorrowed and angered towards what was happening in his father's land.

> *"And it came to pass, when I heard these words, that I sat down and wept, and mourned certain days, and fasted, and prayed before the God of heaven"*
>
> *Nehemiah 1: 4*

This was how Nehemiah got his vision, his passion and his commission to be a channel through which there will be hope, deliverance and honour for his father's land. He could have felt unconcerned and said, 'anyway, I am here, and others could be doing that which concerned Jerusalem'. He caught the vision to change and take the lead when it was needed. Nehemiah later went to his father's land to be the change and to bring that change, having been favoured in every way.

THE OPPRESSOR AND THE OPPRESSED

> *"Yet now our flesh is as the flesh of our brethren, our children as their children: and lo, we bring into bondage our sons and our daughters to be servants, and some of our sons and our daughters to be servants, and some of our daughters are brought unto bondage already: neither is it in our power to redeem them; for other men have our lands and vineyards."*
>
> *Nehemiah 5:5*

The scenario in the above passage confirmed what was mentioned earlier about generational oppression. When lands and vineyards are forcefully taken over by someone else, what is passed down to everyone in that lineage is oppression. When families release their son or daughter because of a debt or similar cause, then, such a people are sold out to slavery and oppression already. This is still happening in different parts of the world.

This was the situation for Nehemiah in the land of his birth and which he tried to a bring change to. How would he be able to bring a change to this lifelong situation and oppression? Some of the reasons for this kind of scenario are famine, poverty, corruption, injustice and ungodliness.

"And I was very angry when I heard their cry and these words"

Nehemiah 5: 6

This was anger in display. However, this was not an anger born out of selfishness, jealousy or oppression. This was a holy anger which was centred on bringing change. This was the anger of a man who wanted to bring change to the land. This was a man who was angry at injustice and oppression among his people. What is your anger directed towards? Be ready, be sure and determined because it is time for a change in your own society and in your nation.

OPPRESSION HINDERS PROGRESS

"Hear, O God; for we are despised..7But it came to pass, that when Samballat, and Tobiah and

the Arabians…, then they were very wroth. 8And conspired all of them together to come and to fight against Jerusalem, and to hinder it. 11And our adversaries said, They shall not know, neither see till we come in the midst among them, and slay them, and cause the work to cease"

Nehemiah 4: 4a, 7, 8, 11

The oppressor will always despise their victims. This is a form of verbal oppression to weaken them - emotionally and mentally. This is one of the tactics of the oppressor by using mental oppression. For example, when the adversaries in the above passage tried mental oppression, they then resorted into tactics of physical attack.

The adversaries even wanted to kill the people. They desired to still place them under bondage and keep oppressing them. Nehemiah was angry at the oppression from within and oppression from outside. He really had a lot to deal with. By the way, are you angry at oppression, at injustice and ungodliness within the society? If not, you may be denying yourself a great possession and treasure.

It is the people that are angry at the status quo that makes a decision to bring change. It is the people who are displeased with injustice that can be a channel for social justice. It is the people who cannot stand oppression that qualifies to fight today's modern slavery. Then, where do you stand on different issues today? You need to take a stand, if only for the sake of posterity.

HOW TO CONFRONT OPPRESSION

1. <u>Take counsel, think and discuss with stake-holders</u>

"Then I consulted with myself ..."

Nehemiah 5: 7

Consider the issue at hand carefully. Discuss widely with the people involved and take a stand. Take caution when needed, pray as someone with an assignment and make decisions towards a solution.

2. <u>Confront logically the officials that are rooted in oppression</u>

"...and I rebuked the nobles, and the rulers, and said unto them, Ye exact usury, everyone of his brother. And I set a great assembly against them"

Nehemiah 5: 7b

Nehemiah campaigned against these people openly. He did this by calling for a public gathering. In today's world, this is called public lecture or campaigning, or organising a peaceful and public protest. So Nehemiah confronted everyone who used their wealth to oppress others. He confronted the government officials using their position or privileges to oppress the people. You can do the same at any level at the moment.

3. <u>State your case lawfully</u>

"I said to them, "To the extent possible we have bought back our fellow Jews, who had been sold

to Gentiles. But now you yourselves want to sell your own countrymen"

Nehemiah 5: 8

Nehemiah stated his case that it was not right for them to do harm or to be a pain to the people, instead they ought to be a comfort. Endeavour to make your point known, as you extract from the constitution, the moral law, the law of God and even the 'conscience law', to support your point.

4. <u>Your wisdom will silence the adversaries</u>

"They were utterly silent, and could find nothing to say"

Nehemiah 5: 8b

When men of wisdom speak, people are bound to listen and comply. Wisdom rules the world and above all, the wisdom of God.

5. <u>Teach them the fear of God</u>

"Then I said, the things that you are doing is wrong! Should you not conduct yourself in the fear of God in order to avoid the reproach of the heathen are our enemies?"

Nehemiah 5: 9

The fear of God is the root of wisdom. With the fear of God, a man will live his life in the direction of God's will. It is not God's will for any man to be oppressed.

6. Warn them of the bad image of society to the outside world

Let them know that their oppressions will bring reproach to society and the nation. Some parts of Africa are known for different vices. Those with precious natural resources are known for certain vices, such as atrocities, oppressions, corruption and injustice. These should be a thing of the past if more people will rise up, speak up and act.

7. Live an exemplary life before them

"Even I and my relatives and my associates are lending them money and grain. But let us abandon this practice of seizing collateral!"

Nehemiah 5: 10

When you live an exemplary life as Nehemiah did, your voice will then be heard much more loudly than ever. In this way and manner, not only will your voice be followed but your lifestyle too. This is the way to make oppression a thing of the past or be brought to the barest minimum. Be the change today!

8. Demand restoration

"This day return to them their fields, their vineyards, their olive trees and their houses along with the interest that you are exacting from them on the money....."

Nehemiah 5: 11

Who is going to be the change and who is going to

bring the change? Let's stand up together and demand restoration of the entire stolen commonwealth. Let's demand that it can no longer be business as usual. Stand up, stand out and be counted with the people that will build the wall of peace and progress and not oppression across the nation.

CHAPTER SEVEN

DEALING WITH THE ROOT OF UNGODLINESS

DEALING WITH THE ROOT OF UNGODLINESS

In front of a house that I have lived as a young boy, there was an orange tree. The small shrub eventually grew to become a big orange tree. In other words, the small root had become a strong tap root with other roots all around it until it became a big orange tree.

The tree was being trimmed when needed and without affecting its roots. One day, the road that passed in front of the house needed to be extended and this tree had to be removed. Therefore, the tree that was only trimmed regularly had become so big that in a short time, it was pulled out of the ground by a caterpillar. That was a big change.

In the same way this tree that had been on the same spot for many years and now uprooted, is the same way ungodliness must be dealt with, wherever it may be found. To do this, like the road that was extended, the pathway of godliness must be expanded, in order to uproot every form of ungodliness in the community, nation, the Church of Christ and society at large.

In every society, it might interest you to know that at the root of every form of ungodliness, injustice, nepotism, selfishness, every rivalry and competitive jealousy, is the monster called greed. Be it from the councillor in the community, the presidential villa, different governmental departments, cutting across the natural sphere and among those who are the custodian of the spiritual kingdom, greed is evident. Greed is an excessive desire for something more than one's proper share.

THE ROOTS OF UNGODLINESS

Greed has been enthroned in different stratum of society, from the lowest to the highest level. It is operating from the political to the financial sphere, from the natural sphere to the supernatural sphere.

There are different types of greed:
1. Greed for power.
2. Greed for wealth.
3. Greed for control and dominance.
4. Greed for pleasure.

These different dimensions of greed are the root cause of ungodliness in every stratum of life today. These are what I refer to as the strong roots holding forth the trees of ungodliness in every strata of society. Therefore, it is time you and I arise with strength and 'weapons' to deal with the roots of ungodliness.

Different 'roots' will be looked into, their impacts in breeding ungodliness and how to deal with them.

GREED FOR POWER

"If thou seest the oppression of the poor, and violent perverting of judgment and justice in a province, marvel not at the matter: for he that is higher than the highest regardeth; and there be higher than they. Moreover the profit of the earth is for all: the king himself is served by the field"

Ecclesiastics 5: 8, 9

Power and its benefits is always what people crave for.

However, so many today go after their passion for power at the expense of fellow citizens.

As a result of this greed for power, the poor is not only silenced but also oppressed. At the same time, there is the perversion of justice of different dimensions. Be it the eviction of people from their land while such people are given little or nothing as a form of compensation for such action. In some cases, they are not even relocated to any particular area.

In 2014, there was a story in the media that made known the eviction of the local people from their land in the suburb of Abuja, the federal capital of Nigeria. These people were protesting their unlawful eviction from their land.

Likewise, people do not take responsibility in the way they ought to for different occurrences in government administration. Occurrences that have direct implication on the people, in the way they are impacted as a result of official actions and inactions. If people in the position of power are not made to be accountable, then, ungodliness, injustice and oppression will continue to be the order of the day in the society.

At the power hierarchy you see around, it seems some people are higher and better than others. Until there is equal and fair portion of opportunities apportioned for every citizen, the power structure may need to be re-structured.

For too long, the people have been insulted by ungod-liness and among the root cause is greed. Individuals with greed for power see others as elements to be op-pressed.

Therefore, no one should be given power and for everything that promotes this greed.

GREED FOR WEALTH

"Wealth is treacherous, and the arrogant are never at rest. They open their mouths as wide as the grave, and like death, they are never satisfied. In their greed they have gathered up many nations and swallowed many peoples. But soon their captives will taunt them. They will mock them, saying, 'What sorrow awaits you thieves! Now you will get what you deserve! You've become rich by extortion, but how much longer can this go on?"

Habakkuk 2: 5, 6 (NLT)

The above Scripture reveals the atrocities being committed as a result of the greed for wealth. Those who go on this path do not consider anything necessary or important to stand on their way to fulfil the desire of their greed for wealth. They amass wealth that generations after them cannot even exhaust. They swallow other people's inheritance and are left with nothing. They place the citizens in captivity as a result of their greed.

According to verse 6, those that put people in captivity place curses upon themselves. This captivity is not outside of their nation but still within their nation. Captivity such as, poverty, mental degradation and psychological trauma, are what these individuals have placed the people under. This is because someone or some people have taken it upon themselves to be ruled by greed for wealth.

Therefore, their evil passion and actions have circulated and spread ungodliness and injustice. Onus now lies on the lap of those that have all these as insults by ungodliness and injustice.

Who is the wise man that will take the responsibility to stand up for the right of the community, the nation and the society in general? This is the way of wisdom. This is the path to take in order to deal with the root of ungodliness in the community, in the nation and in the society.

"for the love of money is the root of all evil"

1Timothy 6: 10

The above Scripture didn't say, 'money is the root of all evil', but it did say, "the love of money...". Therefore, money is never evil but the love of it is evil and is the root of all other evil, such as ungodliness, injustice, crimes and other forms of evil.

This is a product of greed for wealth, which today can be witnessed in the natural field or sphere, and as well in the Kingdom of God.

GREED FOR PLEASURE

In today's world, pleasure has metamorphosed from just being over-eating or other indulgences to becoming an effort to change the creation of God into another un-godly. This is what I called an increasing manifestation of the greed for pleasure.

This is part of the signs of the end time which is greed for pleasure. This is the reason why there is so much un-godliness around and the society has been faced with being insulted by ungodliness. Ungodliness is confront-ing the society and everyone seems to be at its mercy because of greed for pleasure.

"This know also, that in the last days perilous times shall come. For men shall be lovers of their own selves. Traitors, heady, high-minded, lovers of pleasures more than lovers of God"

2 Timothy 3: 1, 2a, 5

One of the main roots of ungodliness is being a lover of pleasure more than a lover of God. When greed is enthroned, be it in a community or nation, ungodliness is celebrated at the altar of human pleasure. Each day, we are insulted by ungodliness. However, it is the attitude and the disposition we have toward this that determines the outcome and the impact on us.

"Put to death, therefore, whatever belongs to your earthly nature: sexual immorality, impurity, lust, evil desires and greed, which is idolatry"

Colossians 3:5 (NIV)

You and I are charged to slay as it were, all things that form greed and its products. In every society, the products of greed are ungodliness, injustice, and every form of vices.

"But now I am writing to you that you must not associate with anyone who claims to be a brother or sister but is sexually immoral or greedy, an idolater or slanderer, a drunkard or swindler. Do not even eat with such people"

1 Corinthians 5: 11 (NIV)

GREED FOR CONTROL

An apprentice who is learning one trade or the other today is doing so just because he would like to be in control of his life tomorrow. There is nothing wrong or contrary with such a goal or an ambition. A desire and a goal not to be subservient to another or to be in charge of one's life is a good thing to do.

However, there are some people today who see as a right to be in control of the community or nation at will. That is, they demand the control over the society in an ungodly manner; this is part of being insulted by ungodliness. Such ungodly acts can be seen not only in the political world but also in the Kingdom of God.

The politicians scheme to control the people because of their greed for controlling the society and the way people think. This is the basic reason why many politicians lie habitually. They make campaign for one thing and they do another thing. In a little while, if care is not taken, politicians are going to turn themselves into objects of worship. Did you think the anti-Christ is going to act alone; he is going to surely come craftily in the clothing of a politician and in the image of a politician.

You and I and society have been insulted by ungodliness for so long and it is time we acted to put a limit, if not an end to the insult of the ungodliness all around us. People are being insulted by ungodliness, injustice and deprived of different kinds of godly human rights. It is to take back the nations for the Lord and enthrone godliness and proper justice in the society.

GREED AT THE PULPIT

"Beware lest any man spoil you through philosophy and vain deceit, after the tradition of men, after the rudiments of the world, and not after Christ"

Colossians 2: 8

Many people out of ignorance of the Word of God are deceived and taken advantage by controlling preachers. The people are taught after the principle of Christ but after the doctrines of men, their belly and their greed.

"From the least to the greatest, their lives are ruled by greed. From prophets to priests, they are all frauds"

Jeremiah 6: 13

This is the reason for the insult at the pulpit because the leaders are ruled by greed. Be it the priest, the pastor or the prophet, all according to the above Scripture, practice fraud. However, even in the New Testament, there is a commandment given by the Apostle on how to lead in the Kingdom of God, let see this:

"Neither as being lords over God's heritage, but being examples to the flock"

1 Peter 3: 5

In other words, the people of the Kingdom of God must not be lord. You are not to try to control their lives because doing such things brings forth other forms of ungodliness. Basically, at the root of such practice is the greed for control.

Different members of the Kingdom of God have been insulted by ungodliness of different kinds as a result of the leadership's greed for control. No one should try to play God over the people that Christ Himself died and resurrected for. The results of such lifestyles by the Kingdom leaders is malpractice, immorality, embezzlement, pride and other forms of vices in the name of God. Here calls for actual focus and standing up against insult of ungodliness even inside the church of Christ.

ARMY OF GODLINESS

When I was growing as a young boy, it was fascinating not only to see soldiers in their well pressed and neat uniform, but also to see them when they were marching in a parade. Our house, at that time as a young boy, was beside an army barrack. Moreover, at a particular hour, the soldiers would blow the trumpets and cornets to play their beautiful music.

Now as an adult, I could understand that soldiers are a well disciplined group of people and they have 'codes' that guide them in everything that they do. In the same way, the army of the Kingdom of God are called and expected to be even more disciplined soldiers:

- They are to represent the heavenly Kingdom in all spheres of life.
- They are to bring orders to the things happening on this side of eternity.
- This army of godliness is to institute and promote order of godliness in the nations.
- This army is expected to deal with every root of ungodliness in the society and bring an end to it.

- This army have jurisdiction in the political world, technical world, financial world and in society at large and in the Kingdom of God.

"And he said unto them, Take heed, and beware of covetousness: for a man's life consisteth not in the abundance of the things which he possesseth. For where your treasure is, there will your heart be also. Let your loins be girded about, and your lights burning; And ye yourselves like unto men that wait for their lord, when he will return from the wedding; that when he cometh and knocketh, they may open unto him immediately"

Luke 12: 15, 34 – 36

This army is expected to overcome and to keep over-coming all forms of greed that may want to cling to them. So likewise they are expected to cut off the influences of such roots in the society at large. In other words, they are expected to cut off the insults of ungodliness and injus-tice over the lives of people in every sphere of influence.

The Lord Jesus taught the people not to allow covet-ousness or greed to take possession of them. He added that a man's life is not qualified by how much wealth, power, pleasure or control he has, but by the values of godliness he possesses. This is what we have been en-joined to make our lives to rally round.

THE DUTIES OF THE ARMY OF GODLINESS

The United States has the greatest and most dynamic army in the world. I state this cautiously and with un-derstanding. This group of people are trained not just to be able to carry out their duties and to adapt to hazardous situation, but they are also equipped to function in different assignments and in different parts of the globe.

In Liberia, for example, from building and doing construction work in resettling the 'ebola' victims, they also encourage the civilian populace in Iraq and Afghanistan to cooperate with them in order to carry out their duties in those regions through different social interactions. Such duties are carried out while still conducting their primary assignment, ie. to combat the enemies of America and the enemies of global peace.

Likewise, in the Kingdom of God, there are duties the army of the Kingdom of God have been called to carry out. In the army of this world, to be at another location while a soldier is supposed to be on duty, is considered a very grievous offence which carries a stiff penalty. How much more it is in the Kingdom of God. In other words, no soldier is expected to be off duty whilst having been drafted into the army of the Kingdom of God.

This army, unlike the armies of this world, serve throughout their earthly sojourn and take upon themselves their responsibilities to the Kingdom of God. The following are the duties of the army of the Kingdom of God:

FIGHTER FOR THE KINGDOM

Everyone who fights always fight with a purpose in mind. For example, as a small child, we may fight to regain our freedom from a bully or to establish our superiority over the competitor. Whatever the reason, it is expected to meet a purpose, whether selfish or not. Nations also go to war to settle superiority between themselves.

However, in the Kingdom of God, you are expected to

fight and to continue fighting to establish and promote the purpose of the Kingdom.

"Let your loins be girded about ..."

Luke 12: 35

It is those who are soldiers that must ensure to have their loins girded. It is for this reason I believe the Lord Jesus commanded His disciples to have their loins to be girded like soldiers. This is because at the loins armours are kept safe and secured. It is only when the armours are secured that a soldier can fight effectively.

"Put on the whole armour of God, that ye may be able to stand against the wiles of the devil. Stand therefore, having your loins girt about with truth, and having on the breastplate of righteousness"

Ephesians 6: 11, 14

What the Lord Jesus commanded was what Apostle Paul repeated in the above Scriptures.

Insults of ungodliness are so rampant in our communities, in our nation and in society that the army of godliness must not give in and become slack in their stand against every ungodliness and injustice. Truth must have its free course in society; the people must be freed from the parade of the onslaught of the devil in our communities.

Many are still under the bondage of the enemy and are still being incapacitated by the works of the enemy. However, with the rising of the army of godliness, the insults of the ungodly will soon be brought to an end. Who will join this army and stand against the insults of ungodliness.

LIGHT OF THE KINGDOM

Light is much more powerful and stronger than darkness both in the natural and supernatural. Therefore, as a soldier of the Kingdom, you must be determined to stand out as the Light in this world filled with darkness and ungodliness.

"... and your lights burning"

Luke 12: 35

As a soldier of the Kingdom, you are a light bearer as well. In other words, you also fight with the Light of God. You possess the Light, so shine forth the light for the world in darkness.

You must be determined to overcome the insults of the ungodliness of this world with the weapon of the Light inside of you. The Light of the Kingdom of God remains the strongest weapon for you to fight with in order to have a continuous victory over the enemies.

If this Light is given priority, we will see victory over the enemies in the political world and in every other sphere of life. Victory over every insult of ungodliness and injustice is possible; in the communities and in the nation, even by dethroning the altars of ungodliness, injustice and wasting of lives and potentials. Therefore as a member of the army of godliness, you must maximize the time and opportunity to keep promoting the truth, purpose and power of the Kingdom of God.

SERVANT OF GODLINESS

Every servant is expected to be committed to his master.

"And the Lord said, Who then is that faithful and wise steward, whom his lord shall make ruler over his household, to give them their portion of meat in due season? Blessed is that servant, whom his lord when he cometh shall find so doing"

Luke 12: 42, 43

A steward in the above Scripture is a servant who serves. In the same way, an army of godliness is expected to serve the people of the Kingdom in all capacity. Whether it is by the teaching of the Word or through prayers and other functions, a soldier of the Kingdom must be willing to serve.

Wherever you are, be ready to create the enabling spiritual atmosphere for the sake of the Kingdom of God. That is, like the motto of the 'Boy's Scout', you must be ever prepared to serve as a member of the army of godliness. The Kingdom of God is depending on you to make the atmosphere more conducive for the purpose of prospering the Kingdom of God.

For example, the activities and the operations of the Kingdom can prosper effectively when there is peace in the land. Likewise:

- When the gospel of the Lord Jesus is not hindered in any way.

- When the community thrives socially and in experiencing justice.

- When godly leaders are in power and they are accountable to the people.

- When righteousness and godliness is enthroned and there is peace on our streets.

"I exhort therefore, that, first of all, supplications, prayers, intercessions, and giving of thanks, be made for all men; For kings, and for all that are in authority; that we may lead a quiet and peaceable life in all godliness and honesty"

1 Timothy 2: 1, 2

In conclusion, godliness is continuously enthroned as the army of the LORD so therefore arise and take your place in this season, especially as we are seeing so much insults of ungodliness. Who will arise and be truly enlisted in the army of the LORD; the army of godliness?

CHAPTER EIGHT

THE PROVOKED GENERATION

THE PROVOKED
GENERATION

Perhaps we have been so much concerned about the negative aspect of anger that we have neglected or forgotten the positive aspect of anger. There is definitely a positive aspect of anger such as, anger at sin and anger at ungodliness or injustice of the society.

King David, Eleazer and Caleb all lived at different times and in different generations. However, they all belong to a common generation of what I call, 'the provoked generation'. This is the generation that got provoked intentionally just because they wanted to make a change for their nation. We will look into these people's lifestyles and study what provoked them and learn from them.

There is no one or group of people that would ever be free from bondage without making room for a change. There is no one or a group that would ever be able to achieve or accomplish anything unique except that they are angry with their situation. That is, there is a need for you or your group to become part of the provoked generation.

The natural earth is governed by the laws of science. In the same way, spiritually, there is a law that governs accomplishment, success, freedom, deliverance and victory, to mention only a few.

What law determines success, deliverance and freedom to mention but a few? The law that governs each one of these could defer, but something is common to all; an individual who wants to attain any of these must have a mindset, a particular attitude and act in a particular manner. A mindset to go for what he desires, an attitude that does not give up and an action that keeps striving for that thing until he attains it. In other words, whatever it is in life that is worth attaining, there must be something that is provoking an individual to go for that thing passionately.

Why do you have to be provoked to prevail in life? It is because the system of this life is programmed negatively. That is, the world is running or being run by ungodliness. This is what you see around you and what is rampant in society. This is why it is mandatory for you to be irritated by the ungodliness around you.

We will look at the principle that allows provocation. That is, I will give you guidelines and case studies of men who were provoked intentionally in order for them to succeed or to remove the barrier over them, prevail over their enemies and the enemies of their nations. In order words, I will try to make it easier for you to get provoked. Yes, to get provoked in a godly manner because there is a godly provocation. Therefore, there is a need for a provoked generation to arise.

With this in mind, I will let you see the characteristics of the provoked generation so that you may be able to look at yourself in the mirror and see what you could look like.

CHARACTERISTICS OF THE PROVOKED GENERATION

THEY DO NOT ACCEPT LIMITATION:

Yes, there are limitations all around us. There are forces in the society and in the nation that want to see the people limited.

It could be the force of politics, the force of oppression, the force of the military or other forces that continually press down the head of the people.

Poverty is a force that pulls down the head of the people. It is only a provoked generation that will be angry and refuse to accept the limitation of such. It could also be the limitation of an individual, the community, the society and the nation. The individuals that will stand or speak or act for the sake of the society must be the kind of people that do not accept limitation.

Malala for example is a part of the provoked generation. She refused to let anybody's gun threaten her or hinder her from seeking education. Moreover, her effort was not only for her but for other girls like her. I saw a young girl who, though her parents were not able to pay her school fees, still went ahead to attend school. The teacher sent her home but she still went back to the classroom the next day.

Some other individuals sent themselves to school regardless of the circumstances of their background. These people were simply angry at illiteracy, angry at poverty and they refused for it to come near them. Likewise, everyone that will stand for others will be advocates against injustice, against ungodliness and oppression. Such an individual must not accept the limitation raised by the enemies of social justice, equity and truth.

THEY SPEAK OUT:

Someone can be provoked to speak. Someone who you never thought could speak out would do so if provoked. Such is the generation of the provoked people.

> *"And as he said these things unto them, the scribes and the Pharisees began to urge him vehemently and to provoke him to speak of many things"*
>
> *Luke 11: 53*

The Lord Jesus was scolding and rebuking the wicked leaders of His days. The Pharisees knew the Lord Jesus was always speaking against their lawlessness, ignorance and corruption. They were trying to hold something against him so they could speak evil of Him in the presence of Herod and the High priest in order to arrest and kill Him. They tried to stir Him, to enrage Him to speak in order to catch him by His words.

The provoked people and the provoked generation are people that speak out. They must speak because they have been provoked. In other words, you are not entitled to stand or speak on behalf of the people or society, except that you are already provoked. Your leadership resumé must describe how many 'provocations' that brings about positive change that you participated in.

How much are you provoked, how effective is your anger? What is the object of your anger or for what reason are you disturbed or perturbed about? You must be able to know what direction or what is the assignment your anger is making you to focus on. You must speak in line with that and must be differentiated by what you stand for.

THEY JOINED FORCES WITH LIKE-MINDED PEO-PLE:

When you are pushed to the wall, you will act and do things you have never done before. This is because you will want to preserve your sanity. Self preservation is one of the needs of mankind. You must also be able to know when to withdraw yourself and to whom you must mingle with. In other words, you must make sure you have a company; your own group that you share a common belief, a common purpose and one mind on most issues, if not all. The provoked generation must be well prepared and you should have people around you that believe in you or believe in each other. That is, the provoked generation must stay, stand, relate and move together like a flock.

However, they may not be in the same location at the same time, but they must stand and stay together in order that their common enemies and the situation they are standing against do not overwhelm them.

"And Gilead's wife bare him sons: and his wife's sons grew up, and they thrust out Jephthah, and said unto him, Thou shalt not inherit in our father's house; for thou art the son of a strange woman. Then Jephthah fled from his brethren"

Judges 11:3

Jephthah was insulted. He was called names; he was called a bastard. He was molested and referred to as someone without a true or genuine identity. Jephthah had to flee from those who could take his life just because of physical inheritance.

Likewise, you need to know what to do you are being irritated and when your life is at stake. Jephthah moved to another location with the people who were also rebellious. The frustrated joined themselves to another frustrated man. The point here is not whether those men were successful or not. They were already unsuccessful people that joined themselves to him. They were described as vain men.

However, the point is to let the provoked ones join the other provoked ones. Let there be a common force through which they will be able to accomplish more than an individual could do.

THEY WILL PAY THE PRICE:

There is a price for everything in life. Even what you receive freely has already been paid for by someone. Those that have been provoked in their generation were either prepared to pay the price or they did not mind what price they would pay. This is the mind-set of the provoked generation. They are prepared to go all the way with their dream of getting angry at what is wrong in society.

If you are really angry, then you must be willing to pay the price of being alone or be remanded for someone else to have their freedom, illumination and justice.

GIDEON AS AN EXAMPLE:

Gideon was a typical example; someone who did not mind to pay the ultimate price if need be in order to obey God and to bring the people back to the Lord.

"Then Gideon took ten men of his servants, and did as the LORD had said unto him: and so it was, because he feared his father's household, and the men of the city, that he could not do it by day, that he did it by night. And when the men of the city arose early in the morning, behold, the altar of Baal was cast down, and the grove was cut down that was by it, and the second bullock was offered upon the altar that was built. And they said one to another, Who hath done this thing? And when they enquired and asked, they said, Gideon the son of Joash hath done this thing. Then the men of the city said unto Joash, Bring out thy son, that he may die: because he hath cast down the altar of Baal, and because he hath cut down the grove that was by it"

Judges 6: 27 – 30

Definitely, Gideon did not die. The Lord was with him as He promised and he brought victory to Israel just because he demonstrated holy anger against ungodliness. There are decisions you will have to make if you are willing to stay on the path of godliness and to be at the fore front of those that will stand against every ungodliness and injustice.

THE REPRESENTATIVES
OF THE PROVOKED GENERATION

CALEB

"And they brought up an evil report of the land which they have searched unto the children of

Israel, saying, the land, through which we have gone to search it, is a land that eateth up the inhabitants thereof,... 30And Caleb stilled the people before Moses, and said, Let us go up at once, and possess it; for we are well able to overcome it"

Numbers 13: 32,30

"...and Caleb the son of Jephunneh, which were of them that searched the land, rent their clothes. 7And they spake unto all the company of the children of Israel saying, The land, which we passed through to search it, is an exceeding good land"

Numbers 14: 6, 7

Caleb, including Joshua, happened to stand out among others. He was simply an angry man. He had his eyes on the Promised Land and on the future and he was not ready to let anyone make futile his conviction at a point where he tore his clothes. To tear one's clothes in ancient time was to be angry, even at the highest level.

Caleb was an example of a provoked man among the other team members – the spies. He was angry at the other people who gave a bad report. He was angry at the generality of the people who refused to believe the Lord's Promise. He seemed to be in the minority, but this is a minority that was right. Why was he right? He was fighting for the Promised Land because that was the very reason he was angry. He was angry that those other ten people gave false reports to the congregation of millions of people. That was a leader who stood for what he knew. That was a man who was a representative of the provoked generations.

In the same vein, you can stand for the truth that you know; stand for your conviction; stand tall among the evil giants who seek to pull down the head of everyone. It is only those that see it as a normal thing for them to be provoked at what is not right around them that they will enjoy the benefits, the privilege and opportunities to possess every mountain, just as Caleb later did.

"... and Caleb the son of Jephunneh the Kenezite said unto him, Thou knowest the thing that the LORD said unto Moses the man of God concerning me and thee in Kadeshbarnea. As yet I am as strong this day as I was in the day that Moses sent me: as my strength was then, even so is my strength now, for war, both to go out, and to come in. Now therefore give me this mountain, whereof the LORD spake in that day; for thou heardest in that day how the Anakims were there, and that the cities were great and fenced: if so be the LORD will be with me, then I shall be able to drive them out, as the LORD said. And Joshua blessed him, and gave unto Caleb the son of Jephunneh Hebron for an inheritance. Hebron therefore became the inheritance of Caleb the son of Jephunneh the Kenezite unto this day, because that he wholly followed the LORD God of Israel"

Joshua 14: 6, 11, 12, 13, 14

These are the benefits and privileges Caleb enjoyed. He got the mountain he desired and enjoyed good health coupled with honour at his old age.

Mountains need to be possessed so that people would no longer live in fear and terror. Why? This is because behind those mountains are the wolves and the devouring lions ready to tear down the people.

Be angry now against what is not right, against ungodliness and injustice. The society is at a crossroad and needs individuals who are really provoked and who can lead the people. Then, there will come forth a company of the provoked generation who will not settle for anything less than what is right and proper. Will you be a part?

DAVID

David, who later became king over Israel, had a phenomenal life. From an early age, he began to take a big responsibility for others. He also had the responsibility of looking after the family sheep. He also had to make sure none of the sheep was eaten by wild animals.

David was a shepherd with a difference. He was a shepherd who confronted and endangered his life for the sake of the sheep. He battled with the lion and the bear and snatched the sheep from their mouth.

He demonstrated his anger towards the lion and the bear which came to eat the sheep. His anger was a demonstration of his love, his care and passion for the sheep. Right from his young age he demonstrated anger towards the enemies of those in his care. He later used the same style or passion to deliver Israel from their enemies.

If you are faithful in little things, then you will be given a bigger commitment. David did not just assume that, "oh its only ordinary sheep let the lion or the bear eat them". David's anger was as a result of his love and care for the sheep. Everyone therefore that will be a leader, a deliverer, an advocate for the oppressed, for those that had no voice and for those whose justice have been taken from them, must have love and passion for those people.

Therefore, for anger to be demonstrated, love must be the reason for it. Moreover, you can only stand up, speak out and fight for the society and nation when you have genuine love and passion for the people. David was a typical and unique man and an active participant among the provoked generations.

'ANGER WITH ACTION'

"Thy servant slew both the lion and the bear: and this uncircumcised Philistine shall be as one of them, seeing he hath defied the armies of the living God"

1 Samuel 17: 36

The anger of David against the enemies of the Lord and His people was born out his love for them and the passion for the Covenant. Your anger against every form of insult and oppression must be out of love. Is your passion about your ambition or selfishness? Every member of the provoked generation must have this to consider.

David saw Goliath like the lion and bear that attacked the sheep. He saw the giant becoming one of them. First, every soldier going to war must have anger towards the enemy. It is that passion that brings the urge, the strength and power to get victory for the people and nation.

What then was the strength of David to face a giant called Goliath? It was because he felt insulted by Goliath. Goliath insulted His God; the Army of the LORD, and also insulted and despised David as a person. The enemies of the society and nation will always want to despise, insult and even suppress every machinery or individuals that could stand as a challenge to their injustice, ungodliness, corruption and oppression.

To make a difference, you have to consciously stand out. You have to know your cause. You also have to stand and take responsibility over every lion, every bear and over the Goliaths of this world. This is because, to be a champion or a representative of the provoked generation, you have to stand over these confronting enemies.

They are the enemies of existence, they are the enemies of productivity, and they are the enemies of freedom and fulfilment. These are the descriptions of the lion, the bear and the giant David slaughtered. One came to attack his responsibilities, another came against his products and the other wanted to take his freedom.

FIGHT FOR YOUR CONVICTION

It should therefore not surprise you that David was angry at all these attackers and giant. It was a battle over being able to protect his freedom and the Covenant.

What are you willing to fight for? Are you provoked already to go for that fight of your life? Speak, stand and act for your society and nation. You do not have to think that someone else would do it. What if you were the one meant to do that. Who could ever think that David was the youngest of the family with his three older brothers on the battle field and would be the one to face Goliath and defeat him?

Stand up for your conviction and face the giant of your life, of your land, of your society and your nation. Every member or representative of the provoked generation must fight because they have been insulted, irritated, oppressed and molested. You have to fight for your family, fight for your community and fight for your nation.

JEPHTHAH

"...and they thrust out Jephthah….. Then Jephthah fled from his brethren…. And Jephthah said unto the elders of Gilead, Did not ye hate me, and expel me out of my father's house? And why are ye come unto me now when ye are in distress? Then Jephthah went with the elders of Gilead and the people made him head and captain over them"

Judges 11: 1, 3 , 7, 11

These elders saw that Jephthah was part of the 'provoked generation' and went after him because they too needed someone who was provoked like them. Moreover, though he was insulted and molested out of his father's house, he refused to give up on life and picked himself up. He then became a champion of the provoked generation.

Perhaps the report of his deeds and exploits got to his people while he was in a foreign land and so they came looking for him. Gilead at that time was already in distress and they were in need of a leader or captain to defend them.

Do not waste your anger. You may just be the candidate to deliver a people from oppression or injustice. The society and entire nation is waiting for such a representative of the provoked generation like you, to rescue, advocate and intercede and stand in the gap to fight for them.

DEBORAH

Without any discrimination, both men and women are members of the provoked generation. Here was a woman who was an example of the provoked generation, who refused to be silenced, who refused to just watch things get worse and stand aloof looking, just because she was a woman.

Deborah was an example of such women. She was a judge in Israel and a Prophetess who led the people of the Lord and who was at her command. She stood in her position, that is, the position that the Lord had placed her in. She took her position when it was time to stand up for the people and to make sure they gained victory over their enemies. There are still sworn enemies confronting the destinies of numerous people today. You can speak out and let your voice be heard and defend them.

"The inhabitants of the villages ceased, they ceased in Israel, until that I Deborah arose, that I arose a mother in Israel. My heart is toward the governors of Israel that offered themselves willingly among the people. Bless ye the Lord"

Judges 5:7,9

Village life ceased in Israel and there was no peace. That was because the heart of the people was filled with fear and uneasiness because of their enemies.

It was in this situation that Deborah arose and stood to take charge. She rose as a judge, as a Prophetess, as a mother and as a fighter in Israel. Taking this charge by Deborah definitely was not without anger. Yes, it was with a positive anger. This was because all those who were to stand up were not interested, timid or unconcerned.

You and I are to be a true member of the provoked generation. This is the people who will not consider their convenience or their background, or any limitation, but who will go beyond the limit. Stand out and be counted now, because of posterity.

CHAPTER NINE

THE SPIRIT OF GODLINESS

THE SPIRIT OF GODLINESS

I have participated and engaged myself in farming at my younger age. Therefore, I have known the importance of hard work. For example, I know that when one prepares a field for planting and removes the weeds, one needs to make sure you do not leave the field like that for a long time. This is because the weeds will surely grow back. This renders the first effort to be wasted and fruitless.

In other words, having removed the roots of the weeds, new crops must be planted. The new crops are now the new occupiers of that field.

In this same vein, since the roots of ungodliness have been dealt with in the previous chapter, we will now look at how to make good planting of godliness on the land.

We will also compare godliness and ungodliness and see the trend of godliness and that of ungodliness in the society.

SPIRIT OF GODLINESS

Just as I mentioned earlier, you need to plant after the weeding. Have you heard that the spirit of someone or something is on a person or is a place? Likewise, we need to plant the spirit of godliness in our community, in our city and nation. This is the focus in this chapter is to look into the ways of godliness. It is on this way of godliness that the individual will do the planting of godliness, which is being done by the workers of godliness in order to harvest of the fruits of godliness.

This is how the spirit of godliness will be impacted and embedded into the lifestyle of the community, the nation and society at large. We will also look at products or things that characterises godliness, even as we compare them with ungodliness.

When all these are received, the insults of ungodliness in our nation and society will be uprooted. This is the manner the society will be allowed to reign above the insults of ungodliness. Arise, you children of godliness, for the love of the nation and for the love of the Kingdom of God.

Up until now we have been quiet with the insults of ungodliness. You and I have been insulted by ungodliness but no more.

WAY OF GODLINESS

Some time ago, I drove home from an official trip. I put the home address on the GPS and I had the option to go on a shorter route with tolls or go on a longer route with a partial toll.

I had to choose from these two options; to either go on a longer route with just one partial toll, or to go on a shorter route with couple of tolls. I decided that I wanted to get home on time and opted for the shorter route with couples of tolls, just because I desired to get home on time.

If most people have their way, they would want to get to their destination in the shortest possible time. This is the desire of most people.

However, the way of godliness is not a short route. The way of godliness is a continuous journey and you don't need to go and take a shorter route. It is a life-long journey that must be taken by those that have been insulted by ungodliness and a desire change for their community, their nation and society.

> *"Blessed is the man that walketh not in the counsel of the ungodly, nor standeth in the way of sinners ..."*
>
> *Psalm 1: 1a*

> *"Better to have little, with godliness ..."*
>
> *Proverbs 11: 8a (NLT)*

> *"But thou, O man of God, flee these things; and follow after righteousness, godliness..."*
>
> *1 Timothy 6:11*

> *"For fools speak foolishness, and make evil plans. They practice ungodliness ..."*
>
> *Isaiah 32: 6a*

If there is a construction or a pathway in the spirit to be made, it is the way of godliness. The truth is that if you do not join the way of godliness, then you do not have any reason to complain when the ungodly are busy planning and making the pathway of ungodliness. The people and the society will then be insulted by ungodliness without any reservation. This is the manifestation of what you and I are seeing today.

PLANTING OF GODLINESS

It is time we begin to plant godliness in every home, on every street, in every community, in every city, in every nation and every available 'field'.

Enough of being insulted by ungodliness, remove this 'weed' and to begin to plant the seeds of godliness. If the weeds are removed and there is nothing planted, it is the weeds that will keep growing.

> *"...that they might be called trees of righteousness, the planting of the LORD, that he might be glorified"*

> *Isaiah 61:3*

Planting of godliness must be a continuous thing. However, one needs to start the planting of godliness from the home front.

> *"...their first responsibility is to show godliness at home"*

> *1 Timothy 5 :4a*

The above Scripture encourages believers to show or display godliness from home. The home remains the foundation of godliness for the society. When the home-front is established, then the nation is on the path of godliness.

Onus lies on every individual who has been insulted by ungodliness to take upon themselves the responsibility to begin to plant seeds of godliness in every available field for the sake of the Kingdom of God. It is all for the love of the future generation and for the love of the Kingdom of God.

"...and exercise thyself rather unto godliness."
1Timothy 4: 7b

The above Scripture reveals how believers need to be trained in godliness. What does it mean to be trained in godliness? Training in godliness is to develop godly characteristics and to be spreading the doctrine or the spirit of godliness.

It is also to educate the home, the community, the legislatures, all leaders and the nation as a whole in godliness. By so doing, when each one sees ungodliness, everyone will be able to recognize it. Also, the propensity of the insults of ungodliness in the society will be reduced.

WORKERS OF GODLINESS

During the inauguration of a former president of Nigeria, he was quoted to have told the Ministers of the gospel of Christ that graced the occasion, something like; *".... We will begin to appoint our own prophets"*.

Someone should tell me when it has now become the responsibility of a president of a nation to begin to appoint his own prophets? However, that is the kind of spirit of ungodliness you see when the people who are supposed to be the custodians and leaders of the Kingdom of God, refuse to stand their ground. Perhaps they have lost it.

Lost what? The true Word of the LORD, the power of God and the boldness to reply, "Sir that definitely is not your responsibility, with all due respect". Whether he meant it or not, that indeed was an affront and a demonstration of an insult of ungodliness.

This is ungodliness insulting us at the face. We have indeed been insulted by ungodliness for too long. It is time we arise and stand for that which is true and just, those who can make the society to prosper and move towards the influence of the Kingdom of God.

Who are then the workers of godliness who will take it upon themselves to stop the workers of ungodliness in the land?

"If any man teach otherwise, and consent not to wholesome words, even the words of our Lord Jesus Christ, and to the doctrine which is according to godliness"

1 Timothy 6:3

This is the responsibility for each and every one who is a leader in one way or the other; whether in the home, in the community, in the corporate world, in the political world and in the Kingdom of Christ. Why would this be so? In order that through the influence of the doctrine of godliness being propagated by these workers of godliness, we will be able to stand against the insults of the ungodliness in the society.

UNGODLINESS CONFRONTED

"Teaching us that, denying ungodliness and worldly lusts, we should live soberly, righteously, and godly, in this present world"

Titus 2: 12

These are ways to confront ungodliness; to shun every deception and enticement of ungodliness, and to keep standing against every form of ungodliness around us. Daily we are being insulted by ungodliness, but if we will arise as workers of godliness and take our place in the kingdom of godliness, then ungodliness and its influence would fade in our society.

FRUITS OF GODLINESS

From my teens, I have always loved to keep flowers. Every time I see those flowering plants growing and showing evidence of fruitfulness, there is a pleasure and satisfaction I derive from it. A fruit that comes forth is the desire and joy for the labour of a farmer.

For everything that is planted, there comes a time for the harvest. The harvest is therefore the fruits, which is the expectation of every one that plants one thing or the other.

Likewise, there are fruits of godliness expected in every labour of godliness. What then are these fruits to be expected and what are the evidence that we should look for in order to confirm the impact of godliness in society.

EVIDENCES OF THESE FRUITS

• **Power:**

Having been translated from the kingdom of darkness into the Kingdom of Light, there are fruits to confirm this translation being carried out.

"According as his divine power hath given unto us all things that pertain unto life and godliness, through the knowledge of him that hath called us to glory and virtue:"

2 Peter 1: 3

We have been given the power needed to live in godliness and to overcome every form of ungodliness around us. Even as you and I receive the needed knowledge, understanding and wisdom to carry this out, it is evident that this scenario is a declaration of war against ungodliness, since ungodliness has always declared war on godliness.

Therefore, by the spirit and the power of godliness, you can overcome every insult of ungodliness. Our society does not have to be continually insulted by ungodliness.

• Profit:

In every trading, there is an expectation of profit. Likewise, in the spiritual transaction, there are profits that are legally expected to accrue to you and me. What is required is to carry out this kingdom transaction in accordance with Kingdom principles. This is your assignment and my assignment. It is evident that this godliness fight, justice campaign and fear of God revolutionary campaign, even among our youths and society in general, will surely make godliness profitable to all.

"For bodily exercise profiteth little: but godliness is profitable unto all things, having promise of the life that now is, and of that which is to come."

1 Timothy 4: 8

• Peace:

When people pray, the community, city and nation can be brought to a low level and stop the insults of ungodliness and injustice. This is when the people of the Kingdom of God lift up their voices and hands in prayer to the LORD. You are to call upon the LORD for your community, your city and for your nation, if you truly want a godly change in the land.

"For kings and for all that are in authority; that we may lead a quiet and peaceable life in all godliness and honesty."

1 Timothy 2: 2

Peace in our city and nation will surely promote the expansion and the establishment of the principles of godliness. It is when justice and godliness thrives that you will be able to have room for peace. It calls for the Church to stand their ground to promote the principles of the Kingdom, in order that our societies stop being insulted by ungodliness.

• Prosperity:

Where the spirit of godliness is, where there are godly principles in action, where there is justice and peace, there will surely be prosperity. This is among the fruits that you and I will see in the society and when these are in operation.

"...Your godliness will lead you forward, and the glory of the Lord will protect you from behind"

Isaiah 58: 8 (NLT)

The nation will experience progress and prosperity in the true sense of it, when the people embrace godliness and justice and when they are no longer insulted by ungodliness in the way they have always been for decades. This is part of the evidences of the fruits of godliness.

DISCOVER THE DIFFERENCE

There are shadows of godliness that will try to look like godliness but they are not. Therefore, those that are of the true spirit of godliness must not only stand their ground, but they must also stand out. There are those that possess the form of godliness, but without the spirit of godliness.

"Having a form of godliness, but denying the power thereof: from such turn away."

2 Timothy 3: 5

Anyone with a form of godliness is promoting ungodliness, whether ignorantly or knowingly. In other words, the group of people that are insulting the society with ungodliness are those that are out rightly known with ungodliness and those that try to mimic godliness. However, the basic element that will distinguish those that are for godliness from those that are promoting ungodliness is if such individuals possess the spirit of godliness and not just a form of it. It is this spirit of godliness that will bring forth the attributes, the principles and the life style of godliness.

CHARACTERISTICS OF GODLINESS

"And without controversy great is the mystery of godliness: God was manifest in the flesh, justified in the Spirit, seen of angels, preached unto the Gentiles, believed on in the world, received up into glory."

1Timothy 3:16

Godliness is not just a doctrine, a belief or a principle, it has a personality. The Lord Jesus is the personality of godliness who came to dwell among mankind. Therefore, to embrace the spirit of godliness is to embrace everything godliness stands for.

Godliness has already come in human flesh to rescue humanity from its own ungodliness. He was justified and empowered by the Holy Spirit to actualize His assignment. Then, the message of godliness is preached unto nations and received.

Learning and taking cue after the above Scriptures:

• The lifestyle must be lived before the people by the children of the Kingdom of God.

• The teaching of godliness must be preached and taught in every available medium.

• The principles of godliness must be ensured to be received by all in the community, city and the nation, even by the young and old.

• The principle of godliness must be believed and embedded as the culture to live by.

• Godliness must be presented with its profit and incentives, not only for the good of the nation and society, but of eternal value.

This is the spirit of godliness. This is the way of life for development, progress and profit for the nation and the society. This is for the good of the people; peace of the society; the nation's development; advancement of the things that really matter for the people such as justice and development, and for the promotion of the Kingdom of God. Join me in this fight against ungodliness as we embrace and promote the spirit of godliness.

CHAPTER TEN

THE SYNERGY
OF SIGNIFICANCE

THE SYNERGY
OF SIGNIFICANCE

Synergy is the cooperation of two or more muscles, nerves or the like.

If you have been insulted by ungodliness, if you happen to be privileged to be irritated by injustice around you, in the society and in the nation, then you are on the right path. In other words, your anger towards ungodliness, towards injustice and the likes, will create a hunger in you to fulfil a particular purpose meant for you.

Moreover, your anger and fury at ungodliness and injustice around you is a licence given to you to fulfil a purpose. That is, those irritations and uneasiness you are faced with are evidence that you have an assignment to fulfil.

Therefore the fulfilling of that purpose will result in something more than you. This is what is called significance. Significance therefore is what you become to the society and to the nation.

The two 'muscles' here are; what irritates you or your anger on ungodliness, and the purpose you are meant to fulfil as a result of the insults by the ungodliness and the likes. This is the synergy that leads to significance. That is, you begin to make a difference and are a force to reckon with.

Everyone desires significance but not everyone is ready to go through the process of being 'pregnant' with the requirements that would make them to be significant. These we will look into. Welcome to a life of being insulted by ungodliness in order to make a difference.

Actually, each individual needs to be pregnant with the seed of purpose. This seed must be acquired through the discovery of it. That is, you have to discover what makes you different in your society. Find out what you need to do to express your importance. This is what will give you significance in life.

THE COMBINATION

Putting the two forces of anger and purpose together is what produces an effect that brings relevance, which is known as significance. It will be good then to look into what and how you can come into significance. This is the essence of life.

This is what is worth living for, what is worth standing for; this is what is worth dying for if need be. Until an individual discovers this, it will be difficult for his life to really have a true meaning. This chapter will be the rounding up of the journey we have been on in this book. Don't waste your anger; likewise don't waste your living as well. This is because a person could waste an important part of his living if he refuses to come into significance; if he refuses to impact lives around, the family and in the community or in the society.

We will look into what could make you step into significance.

DISCOVER YOUR SIGNIFICANCE

Discovery is everything. Yes, what you discover valuable to you can make all the difference in your life. What is it worth discovering, if indeed discovery is everything? If it is only one thing in life that you have or allowed to discover, then it must be your significance.

Someone was said to have discovered the river Niger. Someone was said to have discovered different drugs in medicine that has benefited millions today.

You need to discover something that will impact humanity. Discover what you need to do to make your life have meaning.

For your life to have meaning is to discover what you are meant to fulfil. Are you angry at something that has to do with what others are going through or what others could have access to that you think you could be a channel for? Then press into that. Press into it because that is most likely what could give you significance.

When what you are insulted by meets what you have a strong desire to do, then that would bring you significance. You are on the path of making a difference in the society and in your generation.

"Life is short. It's easy to waste and hard to use" (Michael Stege)

Life span has increased in this century in different parts of the world, either as a result of eating the right kind of food or as a result of medicine and pharmacy. However, with that advancement and progress, not many people are ready to come into full significance of their lives. That is, the life span of today could be 100 or 95 or even 120 years, it is still short compare to eternity.

It is a good thing to live long but it is much more important to make a difference in life by living a life of significance. It is hard to live this kind of life because a life that is actually lived is one that is with significance.

However, it is easy to waste such a life and to waste such a life will have no significance at all.

It is time therefore that you and I live a significant life by impacting one person and even millions of souls. That is, when you are living for something bigger and greater than you, this is living for eternity. When you live for the purpose of making a difference for the people, for society, for the things that are beyond you, then significance will not be able to elude you.

Therefore, when you have discovered your significance, your life will now begin to move towards making a difference. Stay on this path; understand that what you have discovered moves you and what your life should revolve around is more than you. It is in doing that you will find fulfilment; living for others, be other people's eyes, other people's hands, their feet and their mouth. This is what you are furious about, that you do not want to see people lack and that you offer yourself for them. Then you have found your path to making a difference. When you have these in your possession, then welcome to a life of significance and greatness.

PURSUE WHOLENESS

Life is a race. However, it is not a hundred meters dash but a relay race. It is indeed a very long race which you have to be prepared for. What you pursue is what you are running after.

Wholeness implies something that is entire, full, accomplished and fulfilled. This is the type of life the Prince of Life Himself desires you and me to live. However, you can only live this kind of life when you have discovered your significance and you are on the path of pursuing it. It is a life of dedication and commitment. On the path just like the relay race, you may be tempted to opt out but never give up.

Be prepared to be on the race to fulfil and to achieve fulfilment. Keep pursuing it and that which insults you, that which you are angry at in the society and that which you have a passion for, keep following after it and then significance is sure.

In the pursuit of wholeness, there will surely be challenges but you need to keep going. In other words, on the journey unto significance which comes through being whole in all things, challenges will crop up. However, because you are determined and have a conviction about the path that you are on, you will always come out on top.

Discouragement will arise but what you know will keep you moving. This is because you are involved in what is bigger than you and as you are in the centre of God's will, you will impact lives around you.

To have wholeness does not mean you will feel happy all the time. Remember, happiness is determined by what is happening around you. However, your purpose is more than just being happy, but it's about making others to be blessed and happy. Maybe the people you are sent to impact may not be encouraged, but you need to encourage yourself especially if you know you are on the path of significance.

There may also be set backs in one way or another. One thing you must always remember is that you are not alone. It is my opinion and belief that when you have set your heart to do that which God has planned, He will be there with you.

One thing is certain, don't lose track of where you are going and don't lose focus of your goal. Let the people you are sent for be at the back of your mind. This is because it is all about the people that you are sent for according to God's purpose for your life. It is all about getting your life to the level of fulfilment which is wholeness for any man. That is, when your life gets to the stage of being mindful and concerned with impacting and blessing lives, then you are pursuing wholeness as an individual.

LIVE INTENTIONALLY

Life is to be lived and living life is not a day's journey. You came alive in the womb and after being giving birth to, you keep on living in this natural world. However, with about 7 billion people on the earth today not everyone is living intentionally.

Have you ever asked yourself what it takes to stay alive on a daily basis? One, to stay alive on a daily basis, you have to make sure you are breathing and breathing well. You also have to make sure you that every part of your body is active and you stay hydrated.

In other words, you must make sure you possess determination to stay alive daily, weekly, monthly and yearly. You must keep doing everything that would help you to stay alive and strong. This is having the will to live on the inside of you; this is what I refer to as living intentionally, on the physical and physiological level.

However, there is something much more than this. You have to live intentionally as one with a unique purpose and determination. In other words, you have to find out what drives you, what could help you to reach your set goals and what could aid your journey to significance.

It is when you know all these that you would be able to put them all together and use all these information to live intentionally.

After you have made the discovery of your own significance, you would then be able to find the reason to stay alive. Though not just to stay alive physically but to stay alive on the path of significance. This is what happens when you are on the path of making your life have meaning; it makes it count for others.

At this level, you will begin to have the consciousness of those you are to reach; the children you are to feed, the souls you are to preach to and the lives that needs to be touched. This is a journey set before you except you will say 'No'. But having gone so far, it is too wasteful for someone to say 'No' when he is on his journey to significance. Welcome to the path of significance even as you are determined to live intentionally.

It is only those that live intentionally that can accomplish and come to the significance meant for them. To live intentionally implies that it is not going to be always convenient but it is what will take you to significance if you do not give up. It will keep you on this path to significance because you have set your eyes on your vision and purpose.

TAKE A RISK

Taking risk is what everybody does daily. They go out on the street, drive on the highway and sit on the seat you are sitting on, is all taking a risk. This implies that you are taking a risk against all odds or against all contrary force that might be envisaged.

Therefore, you neglected and overcame the negative

thoughts that might be telling you; what if there is a danger on the road? What if the car stops working in the middle of the road or what if another vehicle runs into you? These are some of the risks you take daily and how you overcome them all.

However, there is a greater risk but worth more than all those mentioned above. This particular risk is what should govern and control every other risk. This particular risk is concerning your fulfilment and accomplishment, making a difference in life and coming into significance.

Every risk that you take in order for you to come into significance is the greatest kind of risk to take. Every other 'little' risk you take must have this one at the centre of it; the risk taken to be significant in life. This is a risk taken to make a difference in life, in the light of what you are already convinced of, what you are already doing and what you intend to continue to do, for the benefits of humanity and above all to the glory of the Lord.

> *"Many people are passionate, but because of their limiting beliefs about who they are and what they can do, they never take the actions that could make their dream a reality"*
> *(Anthony Robins)*

You do not limit yourself by limiting your belief. Go all the way and let your soul be in what you are doing and there will be no limitations. Keep believing in your goal, believe in your God-given assignment, and in your duty in life to impact a soul, to rescue people from ungodliness and injustice, then you are on the path of becoming part of the significant people.

FIND YOUR OWN COMPANY

Find your own company of people, your company of like-minds on the journey to significance. This could be of tremendous impact for you on your journey to becoming significant. It has been said that; "if you want to go fast go alone and if you want to go far go together".

In other words, you would need to go on this journey with individuals who are either versatile on the journey or have gone on this journey before. This would be a sure synergy for you on the journey to significance because you are not going alone.

"And being let go, they went to their own company, and reported all that the chief priests and elders had said unto them"

Acts 4: 23

The above passage speaks of what Peter and John did after they were released by their persecutors. They went to their own company; the people whom they were doing business with. This is the people that believed the same thing as them; the people that have the same assignment together.

Who are you with? Perhaps you need to connect with someone with the same or related assignment or passion. Perhaps you need a mentor to guide you in your future assignment or in the duty given to you. This could help you to achieve, fulfil and accomplish your assignment with less challenges or difficulties. This could be because you are in the company of someone or some people who already have an idea of the path to your destination.

"Relationships are the oceans in which we find meaning" (Michael Steger)

Finding meaning for life is simply coming into significance because you have been able to accomplish and fulfil your purpose. This is because a life of significance is a life that imparts others; known and unknown to you, whether in your life and beyond your life time.

However, the vehicle that carries you, which makes your journey easier and to go farther is finding you and coming into your own company. This is part of the benefit of having a company of your own and enjoying the synergy that enables you to come into significance. So, take the ride of your life; fulfil, accomplish by becoming a blessing, by being a backbone, by delivering others from the oppressions of ungodliness, injustice and other vices. This is coming to significance.

YOU ARE SIGNIFICANT

My friend, believe in your assignment; believe in your passion, believe in bringing solution to society. When you have come to the understanding of that which you are meant to fulfil; when you know that you know to the extent of committing your life to a just cause, then nothing will be able to stop you.

Believe you are significant. If you have committed all things to impacting a life at a time, or impacting a community or society, then welcome to a life of significance. Believe that your life is not ordinary and never look down on what you can do to impact a life.

Don't waste your anger, don't suppress the urge that

makes you want to reach a life, speak for someone, deliver the helpless and make your life count. This is the essence of life, to put a smile on someone's face. You can be in the vanguard of those that bring a change to the community and to the nation as a whole.

"Never underestimate the difference YOU can make in the lives of others" (Pablo)

Do you know that no one can estimate the great latent power, treasure and ingenuity that are on the inside of you, until you tap into it? Likewise, what you are worth is beyond what you have as financial or material possession, but your worth is in the lives you are able to impact positively. This is the value placed on your life; this is the life of significance.

You are significant so don't waste those resources in you and don't waste that latent power resident in you. Let that passion be loosed and let it focus on bringing change to society, big or small. It could be to leave an indelible mark on someone's life.

For example, you may volunteer your time or energy whether it is to bring a smile to a hungry child or to be a voice to the voiceless.

Your voice could go to where your feet could not go. Your resources could go to where your hands could not reach. You can be the change needed in the society. Let the captive of ungodliness be set free by your efforts.

Let the slaves of injustice be declared free through your fervency. Let the oppressed smile because you came. Let the soul of the hungry bless you because you care.

Look up and hook up to a life of significance and don't

look down on yourself. This is the life of significance lived by those who lived for others - in this generation and in the generation to come.

CONCLUSION

The world can be a different place just because someone like you has received the mandate to make a difference. The comforting word is that what look or seems to be in the minority today can be in the majority tomorrow. This is a result of many like you, who have purposed to stand with the truth, to stand with godliness, to stand with social justice and equity. This is what you can make happen for the community, for the society and the nation as a whole.

Imagine if the final decision is left to people who have been placing others under bondage and no one chooses to be concerned, what then is going to be the fate of the society. Imagine if you are the one sent or you are the one alive to carry out and fulfil this great mandate. The encouraging truth is that there are many people like you who have been sent to carry out this great assignment.

Where are those who have been irritated by the ungodliness and injustice around them? What are they going to do or what action are they willing to take in order to impact the society? Who is going to take the responsibility to be a game changer for this generation?

My friend, this is the time to get uncomfortable with ungodliness, get irritated with social injustice and be stirred up within you to make a difference at all cost for the good and advancement of the society and the nation.

This is the journey for those who will be irritated and angry at ungodliness; for those who will receive the mandate and the power to bring positive change at all cost; for those who have decided to fight the good fight to bring freedom to the people; for those who will reform the society and the nation; for those who have purposed to stand for something meaningful in life; for those who will refuse oppression in the society; for those who will stand up as the army of godliness to root out the influence of ungodliness; for those who belong to the provoked generation and will defend godliness and its principles; for those who will embrace and celebrate the spirit of godliness in order to plant and establish god-ly attributes, principles and lifestyles in society and for those who have decided to make a significant impact to the society.

This is the journey; this is the path to take which has been tested and traveled by others before us. This is the path to fulfilment and happiness. This is living a pur-poseful life indeed. This is the life worth living. Do you not want to be a part of this? Please join me!

ABOUT PASTOR SUNDAY ADELAJA

Sunday Adelaja is the founder and senior pastor of the Embassy of God in Kiev Ukraine and the author of more than 300 books which are translated in several languages including Chinese, German, French, Arabic, etc.

A fatherless child from a 40 hut village in Nigeria, Sunday was recruited by communist Russia to ignite a revolution, instead he was saved just before leaving for the USSR where he secretly trained himself in the Bible while earning a Master's degree in journalism. By age thirty-three he had built the largest church in Europe.

Today, his church in Kiev has planted over a thousand daughter churches in over fifty countries of the world. Right now they plant four new churches every week. He is known to be the only person in the world pastoring a cross cultural church where 99% of his twenty five thousand members are white Caucasians.

His work has been widely reported by world media outlets like Washington Post, The wall street Journal, Forbes, New York times, Associated Press, Reuters, CNN, BBC, German, Dutch, French National television, etc.

Pastor Sunday had the opportunity to speak on a number of occasions in the United Nations. In 2007 he had the rare privilege of opening the United States Senate with prayers. He has spoken in the Israeli Knesset and the Japanese parliament along with several other countries. Pastor Sunday is known as an expert in national transformation through biblical principles and values.

Pastor Sunday is happily married to his "princess' Pastor Bose Adelaja. They are blessed with three children, Perez, Zoe and Pearl.

Follow Sunday Adelaja
On Social Media

Subscribe And Read Pastor Sunday's Blog:

www.sundayadelajablog.com

Follow These Links And Listen To Over 200 Of Pastor Sunday's Messages Free Of Charge:

http://sundayadelajablog.com/content/

Follow Pastor Sunday on Twitter:

www.twitter.com/official_pastor

Join Pastor Sunday's Facebook page to stay in touch:

www.facebook.com/pastor.sunday.adelaja

Visit our websites for more information about Pastor Sunday's ministry:

http://www.godembassy.com
http://www.pastorsunday.com
http://sundayadelaja.de

CONTACT

For distribution or to order bulk copies of this book,
please contact us:

USA
CORNERSTONE PUBLISHING
info@thecornerstonepublishers.com
+1 (516) 547-4999
www.thecornerstonepublishers.com

AFRICA
Sunday Adelaja Media Ltd.
Email: btawolana@hotmail.com
+2348187518530, +2348097721451,
+2348034093699.

LONDON, UK
Pastor Abraham Great
abrahamagreat@gmail.com
+447711399828, +44-1908538141

KIEV, UKRAINE
pa@godembassy.org
Mobile: +380674401958

Best Selling Books by Dr. Sunday Adelaja

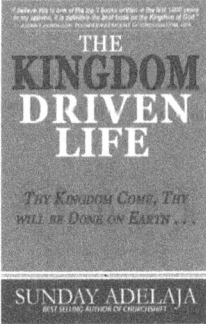

The Kingdom Driven Life:
Thy Kingdom Come, Thy
Will be Done on Earth
(Best seller)

Myles Munroe:
... Finding Answers To Why Good
People Die Tragic And Early Deaths

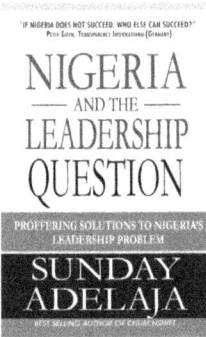

Nigeria And
The Leadership Question:
Proffering Solutions To Nigeria's Leadership Problem

Olorunwa (There Is Sunday):
Portrait Of Sunday Adelaja.
The Roads Of Life.

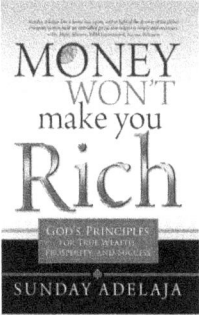

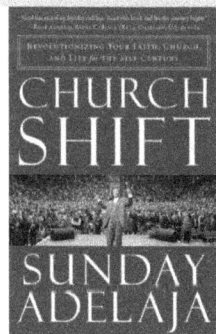

www.ingramcontent.com/pod-product-compliance
Lightning Source LLC
Chambersburg PA
CBHW022130080426
42734CB00006B/297